S 30.162 s

9674

C000258196

Paul and Thomas Su....,

FIG. 1 Francis Cotes (1726–70), *Portrait of Paul Sandby*,
c. 1760. Oil on canvas. Tate Gallery, London

LUKE HERRMANN

Paul and Thomas Sandby

B. T. BATSFORD LTD · LONDON
IN ASSOCIATION WITH THE
VICTORIA & ALBERT MUSEUM

Copyright © Luke Herrmann 1986
First published 1986

All rights reserved. No part of this publication
may be reproduced, in any form or by any means,
without permission from the Publisher

ISBN *0 7134 4788 5 (cased)*
0 7134 4789 3 (limp)

Typeset and printed by Butler & Tanner Ltd,
Frome and London
for the publishers
B. T. Batsford Ltd
4 Fitzhardinge Street
London W1H 0AH

TO THE MEMORY

OF MY PARENTS

Series general editor:
John Murdoch, Deputy Keeper
of the Department of Paintings.
Victoria & Albert Museum

Contents

List of illustrations

Black-and-white

This list does not include illustrations in the catalogue of works in the collection of the Victoria & Albert Museum.

Colour plates *between pages 64 and 65*

Numerals printed in **bold** type in the introductory chapters are references to items in the catalogue. References such as 'fig. 9' indicate illustrations in the general chapters.

Foreword

My interest in Paul Sandby began while I was working on the catalogue of the British drawings at the Ashmolean Museum, and was encouraged by my discovery of the two important early drawings of Leith in the Sutherland Collection (see fig. 3). While writing *British Landscape Painting of the Eighteenth Century* it became clear to me that Sandby was one of the more eminent artists examined in that book who were very much in need of reappraisal, and I began my further work on him in 1974 while enjoying a term as a Visiting Research Fellow at Merton College, Oxford; I would like to take this opportunity of thanking the college for their generous hospitality. It was during that term that I decided that a study of the work of Paul Sandby had to include a study of the drawings of his elder brother, Thomas. Thus this volume has become *Paul and Thomas Sandby*, for when I was invited to undertake it by John Murdoch in 1980 it happily emerged that the V & A collection has just enough drawings by Thomas to make it feasible to include both brothers in this monograph catalogue.

The Sandby brothers have been the subject of two full biographies, both of which are, alas, somewhat unreliable and eccentric. *Thomas and Paul Sandby – Royal Academicians*, by William Sandby, Thomas's great-grandson, was published in 1892. Much more recently, in 1985, the late Dr Johnson Ball's long-awaited *Paul and Thomas Sandby – Royal Academicians* has been published with the intriguing sub-title *An Anglo-Danish Saga of Art, Love and War in Georgian England*. The latter abounds in genealogical detail, and reconfirms the correct birth dates of the brothers, which Dr Ball had first re-established in his Nottingham thesis in 1964. Neither of these books provides a firm basis for a study of the art of the two brothers, and the introductory sections of the present book will attempt to make good that hiatus, something that has not been attempted at any length since the publication of Paul Oppé's invaluable work on the Sandby drawings at Windsor Castle in 1947.

The first major exhibition devoted to the work of the Sandbys was held at the Nottingham Castle Museum in 1884. This was organized with the help of the artists' future biographer, William Sandby, and the majority of the exhibits came from his collection. The next Sandby exhibition came over seven decades later and was an unscholarly assembly of some 160 items at the Guildhall Art Gallery in London in the summer of 1960. Another twelve years later, in 1972, a similar but rather smaller exhibition was shown at the art galleries in Reading and Bolton. In 1977 London saw another Sandby exhibition – 'Etchings and Aquatints by Paul Sandby' – arranged by the William Weston Gallery, who published a most useful small catalogue. There have so far been two Sandby exhibitions in the 1980s, neither of them in England. The first was shown in 1981 and 1982 at four galleries in Australia, having been initiated by Julian Faigan, then Director of the City of Hamilton Art Gallery, which itself possesses an interesting group of late bodycolour drawings. The most recent exhibition has been that shown in the spring of 1985 at the Yale Center for British Art, and largely based on the Center's own representative collection of the work of the brothers, supplemented by loans from the Royal Collection and the British Museum. This exhibition was selected and catalogued by Bruce Robertson, who is preparing a thesis on Paul Sandby.

In recent times I have had especially useful discussions on matters concerning the Sandbys with Jane Roberts at Windsor and with Bruce Robertson at Yale, and rather longer ago with Johnson Ball and Bill Drummond. I am most grateful to these fellow-workers for sharing their knowledge with me. I have also received much help from David Brown, John Hayes, Robert Wark, Andrew Wilton and many other students of British landscape painting, and would like to express my thanks to these. Much of my work has been done in print rooms and libraries, and I owe a great deal to their staff, particularly those at the Ashmolean Museum, the British Museum, the Fitzwilliam Museum, Nottingham Castle Museum, the Royal Library at Windsor and the Yale Center for British Art. It is, of course, the Department of Prints, Drawings and Paintings and the Print Room at the V & A to which I owe the greatest debt, and there I have had constant and willing support, especially from Michael Kauffmann, Lionel Lambourne, Liz Miller, John Murdoch, Jill Saunders, Michael Snodin and Chris Titterington. My colleagues in the History of Art Department at Leicester and my own University Library have given me much help, and I have received a grant from the University of Leicester Research Board; I would like to thank all of these, as also the many other friends, colleagues and institutions who have assisted me over the years. A Resident Research Fellowship at the Yale Center for British Art and a Research Grant from the British Academy have been of great assistance in helping me to undertake research in America. My wife and sons have had to live with the Sandbys for more than a decade, and my final and heartfelt expression of gratitude is to them.

*   *   *   *   *

With the publication in 1981 of the *Concise Catalogue of British Watercolours in the V & A* by Lionel Lambourne and Jean Hamilton and the accompanying microfiche, the national collection became more widely accessible, yet it has long been felt that these important holdings should be catalogued in greater depth. Consequently a series of publications was planned that would combine a detailed catalogue of the Museum's holdings on individual artists with an up-to-date monograph on the artist concerned. Some of the leading painters, such as Cozens, Girtin, Turner, Cotman, Cox and de Wint have been the subject of recent exhibitions or monographs, and these have not been included in this series. Instead, the first artists to be treated in this way are Rooker, Varley, Bonington and his followers, Prout, Paul and Thomas Sandby and J. F. Lewis, and an exhibition of each has been planned to coincide with the publication of the book. Further additions to the series are in prospect. The series is edited by John Murdoch, Deputy Keeper of the Department of Paintings.

I Early years 1723-60

Paul Sandby was an active member of the London art world for over half a century, and though out of fashion and somewhat neglected at the end of his long life he has never been forgotten. His elder brother, Thomas, though a more shadowy figure, was also prominent in the worlds of art and architecture in the second half of the eighteenth century, but his reputation has for long been, and still is, at a low ebb. Little survives of the relatively few buildings which he designed, and his influential lectures as Professor of Architecture at the Royal Academy have not been published. His work as a draughtsman has been overshadowed by that of Paul, though recent research has made it clear that Thomas has as much claim to be designated the 'Father of English Watercolour' as does Paul, to whom that title is usually assigned. The V & A collection has more than twice as many drawings by Paul as by Thomas, but there is enough of the elder brother's work to allow for an adequate survey of his career as an artist. These introductory chapters will be concerned with the life and work of both brothers and their contributions to the development of topographical and landscape art in Britain.

Thomas, baptized in December 1723, and Paul, baptized in January 1731, were both born in Nottingham, the sons of Thomas Sandby, a framework knitter, and his wife Ruth Ash, who died in 1742 and 1766 respectively.[1] There is little factual information about their early life and education in Nottingham, and one traditional story that the brothers started an art school in their native town before leaving it must be discounted.[2] However, it is definite that Thomas began his career as a draughtsman while in Nottingham. The drawing in the Carr Album in the V & A collection (**52p**), *Scene in the park of a Continental château*, dates from 1741 or before, and must be one of the earliest surviving drawings from his hand. At this time Thomas was engaged in making drawings of buildings in Nottingham and of views of the town which were engraved for Charles Deering's elaborate *Nottinghamia Vetus et Nova, or, An Historical Account of the Ancient and Present State of the Town of Nottingham*, though this was not published until 1751.[3] These engravings are somewhat naïve and stiff, as is the large pen and ink view of *Nottingham Market Square from the West* in the Nottingham Castle Collection, which also dates from about 1740.[4] A much more convincing early drawing, which is signed and dated 1741 and which is also at Nottingham,[5] is the elaborate pen and ink *Old Town Hall, Nottingham*, which demonstrates the young Thomas Sandby's mastery of perspective and of other aspects of architectural draughtsmanship at this time. The same qualities are to be found in the much more imaginative *Scene in the park of a Continental château* (**52p**), which the artist must presumably have copied from a drawing or painting by another artist. Nothing definite is known about Thomas Sandby's artistic training in Nottingham, and though he was said by W. A. Sandby to have described himself as 'self-taught',[6] it seems unlikely that this was the case. In his *Biographical Dictionary of British Architects* Howard Colvin has suggested that Thomas (and later also Paul) was apprenticed to Thomas Peat, of the firm of land surveyors Messrs Peat and Badder, who also set up a school in Nottingham.

The elder Thomas Sandby, father of our artists, died in 1742, and this event certainly contributed to the younger Thomas's decision to move to London, where, in the same year, he was engaged as Military Draughtsman in the Ordnance Office in the Tower of London, a post which he retained for the rest of his life. In 1743 Thomas Sandby was sent to Scotland,[7] and he was certainly in Scotland at the time of the Duke of Cumberland's Culloden campaign in 1745-6. Several drawings made at that time are preserved at Windsor.[8] It seems likely that Thomas Sandby was attached to the staff of the Commander-in-Chief, William Augustus, Duke of Cumberland, by this time, but there is no evidence to support the traditional account that Thomas had already been on the Duke's staff at the time of the Dettingen campaign during the War of the Austrian Succession in 1743. However, Thomas was definitely in the Netherlands during the final stages of that war, for there are drawings by him dated 1747 and 1748 of military encampments at Meldart, Zeeland and elsewhere, at Windsor and in the British Museum.[9] All these military drawings are of a high standard, and prove Thomas to have been a gifted topographical and landscape artist at this time. His use of watercolours is fluent and effective, and of a standard rarely found among British artists at this period.

Nothing definite is known about Paul Sandby's movements from the time of the death of his father in 1742, when he was only 11 years old, until March 1747, when, following in his brother's footsteps, he successfully applied for employment by the Board of Ordnance at the Tower of London. One of the drawings submitted to the Board in connection with his application is in the V & A Collection (**1**), and shows that at this time Paul's draughtsmanship was competent but uninspired, though the copies after prints, mostly by Abraham Bloemart, which he also submitted,

FIG. 2 Thomas Sandby, *Panoramic view across country to
Zeeland* (detail), dated *June 22 1748*. Pen and ink and
watercolour. The British Library, London

demonstrate a much more confident use of pen and ink. In 1747 Paul Sandby was appointed the official draughtsman to the Military Survey in Scotland, which was set up under Lt.-Col. David Watson to make maps of the Highlands, as part of the campaign to restore peace in the area after the rebellion of 1745. Paul Sandby was in Scotland for some five years, and during that period he produced numerous landscape drawings and figure studies which are to be found in many collections. The maps on which he was principally employed are now in the Map Library of the British Library, and show the very high standards achieved by Sandby and his colleagues. It appears that Paul Sandby was largely responsible for the colouring of the fair copy of the map, which is, of course, made up of numerous sheets. William Roy, who was Colonel Watson's assistant on the Survey of the Highlands, described the map of Scotland as 'rather ... a magnificent military sketch, than a very accurate map of a country'.[10]

In the Carr Album (**52a, b,** etc.) there are some 25 small sheets of figure studies executed during Paul Sandby's years in Scotland, most of which are thought to be on-the-spot drawings made in Edinburgh and elsewhere. There are other large groups of similar studies at Windsor and in the British Museum. While many of these figure studies are somewhat basic, others show Paul Sandby's growing abilities in this vein, and serve as an indication of the high standard of figure draughtsmanship that Paul Sandby was to achieve in the central years of his career. In landscape Paul Sandby's development was equally significant during these years in Scotland.[11] As his son, Thomas Paul Sandby, wrote in his obituary of his father,

> perhaps the destination of Mr. Sandby to the Highlands was the source of his eminence as a landscape painter, at least in the formation of his peculiar style, as, though he there saw nature in her wildest form, the necessity under which he lay of attending to particular accuracy in filling up the plans, may be supposed to have formed in him that correct and faithful habit, with which he after viewed and delineated her.[12]

Many of Paul Sandby's Scottish landscape drawings show considerable resemblance to the contemporary work of his brother, and there can be little doubt that Thomas was his brother's teacher, or at least mentor, at this time. What both brothers have in common is an affinity with Netherlandish landscape drawing of the late seventeenth and earlier eighteenth centuries. A comparison of one of the panoramic views drawn by Thomas Sandby in the Netherlands in 1748 (for a detail see fig. 2) with Paul's 1749

FIG. 3 Paul Sandby, *South Prospect of Leith*, signed and
dated 1749. Watercolour, pen and ink, and some in-
dications in pencil, $11\frac{1}{2} \times 15\frac{3}{8}$. Sutherland Collection,
Ashmolean Museum, Oxford

South Prospect of Leith in the Ashmolean Museum (fig. 3), clearly illustrates this point, and many more such comparisons could be made.

From T. P. Sandby's *Memoir* we also learn that while in Edinburgh Paul Sandby became 'acquainted with Mr Bell, an engraver in that city' and 'got some insight into his mode of etching, and himself etched a number of scenes in the neighbourhood, which were done on the spot upon the copper'. Paul produced several series as well as individual etchings of Scottish scenes, both while still in Scotland and after his return to London, but most of these were not in fact published until 1765, and it is not clear for what purpose Sandby was making these early prints, of which the elegant *Forest landscape* reproduced here (fig. 4) is a typical example dating from about 1752. This shows both Dutch and French influences, and it seems possible that Paul Sandby was making such etchings as part of his self-education as an artist. It was not until the 1770s that the making of landscape prints was to become a major factor in his career, though it must be remembered that one of his first actions on his return to London was the etching of the series of eight plates satirizing the work of William Hogarth which appeared in 1753 and 1754.[13]

By the time that Paul returned to London, Thomas's association with the Duke of Cumberland had been ratified by his appointment in 1750 as the Duke's Draughtsman at an annual salary of £100. In 1746, after his victory at Culloden, the Duke, who was George II's favourite son, had become Ranger of Windsor Great Park, and he soon began his major campaign of improvement of the estate, including the development of Virginia Water. Much of the labour involved in this great undertaking is said to have been done by soldiers who had served under the Duke in Scotland. While that traditional account is probably based on fact, it has recently been suggested that there is no evidence to support the long-accepted story that Thomas Sandby was the Duke's architect in the creation of Virginia Water and in other improvements in the Park at this time.[14] This work was probably supervised by the architect Henry Flitcroft (1697–1769), and it was not until much later that Thomas Sandby was concerned with architectural work in the Park. However, the fact that Thomas Sandby was employed at Windsor in his capacity as Draughtsman is proved by five panoramic views of the Park which are still in the collection at Windsor.[15] Paul Oppé has suggested that these large and impressive watercolours, two of which are dated 1752, are the survivors of a set of 'Six Different views

FIG. 4 Paul Sandby, *Forest landscape*, *c.* 1752. Etching, $9\frac{3}{4} \times 7\frac{5}{8}$. Ashmolean Museum, Oxford

of Cranbourne Lodge and Park' which are recorded in the *Windsor Guide* of 1768 as hanging in the Dressing Room of the Ranger's house. Though currently in poor condition, but shortly to be cleaned and restored, these drawings illustrate most convincingly the high quality of Thomas Sandby's work in watercolour in the early 1750s, and they provide further evidence for the theory that Paul's rapid improvement as a watercolour artist at this time was largely the result of following his elder brother's lead.

Thomas took Paul under his wing when he returned to London, and there is evidence that early in 1753 the two brothers lived together in Poultney Street (today Great Pulteney Street near Piccadilly Circus) where they held sketching classes.[16] Further proof of their close collaboration is to be found in the series of eight engraved views of Windsor Great Park which were originally issued late in 1754 and republished by Boydell in 1772. Though the plates of this impressive series are inscribed as drawn by Thomas, it is likely that Paul was responsible for the figures and staffage and possible that he also drew some of the landscape.[17] Paul engraved three of these plates; the others were engraved by François Vivares, William Austin, Edward Rooker, Thomas Mason, and P. C. Canot, all of whom were among the leading London engravers of their day. The large bodycolour drawing of *The removal from the Thames at The Bells of Ouseley of the hulk which became the Chinese Junk on Virginia Water* (**2**) is reminiscent of these engravings in style and quality, and illustrates the high standard that Paul's figure and landscape drawing had reached by the mid-1750s. It seems probable that the Duke of Cumberland commissioned, or at least initiated, the Windsor Great Park series, which seems to have been published privately in 1754, perhaps for the Duke, to whom it was dedicated, as a presentation folio for those interested in his work at Windsor.

Another collaborative undertaking by the brothers was a further set of engravings, *Six London Views*, which though not published until 1766 was initiated in the later 1750s, as is proved by the engraved subscription ticket, which is inscribed *175-* and probably dates from about 1758. In this series, which was engraved by Edward Rooker, the drawings are ascribed to both brothers, an indication that the younger was by now on a more equal footing with the elder. It should, however, be noted at this point that no finished drawings of major buildings in central London which can definitely be ascribed to Paul are known today, while there are many such drawings by or attributed to Thomas. Paul's depiction of the London scene is very largely confined to suburban views, such as those of Bayswater and Greenwich in this collection (**17, 18,** etc.), and it is probable that he contributed only the figures and other staffage to the *Six London Views.*

At about this time Paul Sandby and Edward Rooker were also working together on the etching of three illustrations by John Collins for an edition of Tasso's *Jerusalem Delivered.* These three powerful etchings (fig. 5) illustrate 'scenes of wild fantasy' in a 'bold and turbulent' manner,[18] and indicate, as the earlier Scottish etchings had done, that Paul Sandby was gifted with exceptional powers of imagination. His normal employment as a landscape and topographical artist provided scant scope for these, though they are reflected in the lively nature of many of the figure groups in his topographical drawings. Paul Sandby's satirical prints of the mid-1750s have already been referred to, and his work as a figure artist continued throughout that decade. While the representation of figure studies in the V & A collection is poor, there are rich groups of such drawings at Windsor, Yale and elsewhere. The outstanding figure study in the present collection, *The three daughters of the 2nd Earl of Waldegrave with Miss Keppel and a governess* (**6**), has to be dated to *c.* 1770 because of the age of the girls, but on stylistic grounds an earlier date would be feasible.

So far no really convincing reasons have been put forward to explain the motivation and success of the young Paul Sandby's vicious attack on William Hogarth. This is usually seen as a reaction to the older artist's active opposition to the formation of an Academy in London, but it is difficult to credit that either Thomas or Paul could have been at the van of the movements for an artists' Academy at this very early stage of their London careers. However, it is certain that the brothers were closely attached to the household of the Duke of Cumberland, and that Hogarth's ill-disguised attack on the Duke in his much-publicized painting of 1749-50, *The March to Finchley,*[19] may have been a more direct cause of Paul Sandby's onslaught, and was itself the subject of one of Sandby's most telling anti-Hogarth parodies.[20] The engraving of *The March to Finchley* and other Hogarth prints of this period present vivid portrayals of a variety of London characters, and these must have been well-known to Paul Sandby. In 1760 he himself launched a series of etchings, *Twelve London Cries,* which show something of the influence of Hogarth, especially in the crowded title-page reproduced here (fig. 6). Sandby's *London Cries* also illustrate another influence to which the young artist was exposed at this time, that

FIG. 5 Paul Sandby and Edward Rooker, after J. Collins, *The Forest as Enchanted – Scene from Tasso's 'Jerusalem Delivered'*, c. 1760. Etching, 16 × 20¼. History of Art Department, University of Leicester

FIG. 6 (right) Paul Sandby, *Title Page to the 'Twelve London Cries'*, 1760. Etching, 8¾ × 6¾. Ashmolean Museum, Oxford

of the French school of figure drawing and engraving, several representatives of which were in London during the first half of the eighteenth century, most notably Hubert Gravelot and his pupil Charles Grignion. Though only twelve plates of Sandby's *London Cries* were published, there are drawings for several more sets of street characters, all of which illustrate Paul Sandby's figure drawing at its best.[21]

NOTES

1. Dr Johnson Ball (Ball, 1985, p. 342) tentatively suggests as a surprise conclusion to his 'saga' that Thomas and Paul Sandby's actual father was their supposed cousin, Josias Sandby, Prebendary of Worcester Cathedral (1673–1743).

2. Gandon, p. 186.

3. Several plates from Charles Deering's publication are reproduced in Ball, 1985.

4. Repr. Ball, 1985, pl. 88.

5. Repr. Ball, 1985, pl. 2.

6. W. A. Sandby, 1892, p. 7.

7. In a letter dated 19 April 1743, written from London to George Ayscough of Nottingham, Thomas Sandby wrote that he had been 'appointed by the Board of Ordnance to go along with an Engineer into Scotland . . . . I shall set sail next Thursday'. For the whole letter see Ball, 1985, p. 93.

8. Oppé, 1947, Nos. 150–4.

9. Oppé, 1947, Nos. 155–6; British Library, Ad. Ms. 15968, a–c.

10. See Yolande O'Donoghue, *William Roy, 1726–1790, Pioneer of the Ordnance Survey*, British Museum, 1977.

11. See Luke Herrmann, *Burlington Magazine*, 1964 and 1965. There are good groups of Paul Sandby's Scottish drawings in Edinburgh, at the British Museum, and elsewhere.

12. See Oppé, *Burlington*.

13. Repr. Ronald Paulson, *Hogarth*, 1971, pls. 236–43.

14. I owe this suggestion to the Hon. Jane Roberts, to whom I am greatly indebted for discussing her Thomas Sandby researches with me.

15. Oppé, 1947, Nos. 111–15.

16. See E. H. Ramsden, 'The Sandby Brothers in London', *Burlington Magazine*, LXXXVIII (1947), p. 17.

17. In a recent lecture at Yale, Bruce Robertson suggested that Paul was responsible for drawing the entire compositions.

18. Patrick Conner, *Michael Angelo Rooker*, 1985, p. 23.

19. The painting of *The March to Finchley* is in the collection of the Thomas Coram Foundation, Brunswick Square.

20. Repr. Ronald Paulson, *Hogarth*, 1971, pl. 242.

21. There are large collections of *London Cries* drawings at Yale and in the Museum of London; see Robertson, 1985, No. 48.

II Years of success 1760–70

The year 1760, which saw the accession to the throne of George III, a young king who was known to be sympathetic to the arts, was additionally important in the London art world for it saw the first public exhibition of the Society of Artists of Great Britain. Paul Sandby showed five works at this exhibition, of which two were oil paintings, including as No. 54 *A view of Lord Harcourt's Seat at Newnham*, which was very probably one of a pair of impressive large canvases rediscovered a few years ago. Now entitled *Nuneham from the Lock Cottages – Morning* (fig. 7), it shows the recently completed Harcourt 'villa', built between 1756 and 1760, with the Thames and its wooded banks in the foreground. The other canvas, *Oxford from Nuneham – Evening* (which was not exhibited), provides an evocative record of the 'river prospect' which was an important element in the placing and design of the new house. In the context of British landscape painting in 1760 – George Lambert was near the end of his career and Richard Wilson had only returned from Italy some three years earlier – these two canvases were outstanding works.

Unfortunately Paul Sandby's major exhibit of 1761, *An Historical Landskip representing the Welsh Bard in the Opening of Mr. Gray's Celebrated Ode*, is now lost. It seems probable that this ambitious historical landscape had been painted in response to – and in rivalry with – Richard Wilson's *Niobe*, exhibited and well-received in the previous year, and engraved by William Woollett and published by John Boydell with enormous success in 1761. It was to Sandby's canvas, which he himself appears to have commissioned, that the Reverend William Mason was referring in a well-known passage in a letter to Lord Nuneham (later 2nd Earl Harcourt) written in November 1760:

> Sandby has made such a picture! such a bard! such a headlong flood! such a Snowdon! such giant oaks! such desert caves! If it is not the best picture that has been painted in this century in any country I'll give up all my taste to the bench of Bishops.... In a word Sandby improves as much in painting as your Lordship does in caprice, ... and in short time will be that Claude Lorraine, that Browne assured him he was at Lord Scarbro's in my hearing, and therefore desired him not to spoil a Claude by eating too many filberts.[1]

Further praise of Paul Sandby's landscape painting at this time is to be found in another famous passage from a letter, this one written by Thomas Gainsborough to Lord Hardwicke in about 1764, declining a commission to paint '*real Views* from nature in this Country', and recommending Paul

FIG. 7 Paul Sandby, *Nuneham from the Lock Cottages –
Morning*, c. 1760. Oil on canvas, $38\frac{1}{2} \times 58$. Private
Collection, England

Sandby as 'the only Man of Genius, he believes, who has employ'd his pencil that way'.[2]

A further impressive example of Paul Sandby's work in oils at this period has recently been acquired by the British Art Center at Yale.[3] This is an extensive view of Hackwood Park in Hampshire, painted for the 5th Duke of Bolton and exhibited at the Society of Artists in 1764 (No. 101). This canvas is much lighter in tone and more confident in technique than the two Nuneham views, and can be taken as an indication of the high standard of Paul Sandby's landscape painting in the later 1760s. It is reasonably certain that a large proportion of his exhibited work at this time (he showed annually at the Society of Artists) was in oils, but very few of these canvases are known today, and it is not possible at present to make a fair assessment of Paul Sandby as a landscape painter in oils in the earlier part of his career.

The surmise that he had established a reputation as such is supported by the fact that Paul Sandby was one of the twenty-two artists who signed the Memorial presented to George III on 28 November 1768, which led to the foundation of the Royal Academy a few days later, on 10 December. Paul became a member of the Council, while Thomas, who had not signed the Memorial, was named as one of the additional Founder Members and was elected Professor of Architecture on 17 December. We know only the barest outlines of the lives of the brothers in the 1750s and '60s, and Thomas is an even more shadowy figure than Paul. It is recorded that he was appointed Deputy Ranger of Windsor Great Park in 1765, though whether by Duke William Augustus before his death that year, or by his nephew, Henry Frederick, who succeeded him both as Duke of Cumberland and as Ranger of Windsor Great Park, is not known. Duke Henry Frederick was the fourth son of Frederick, Prince of Wales, and at this time was on good terms with his elder brother, George III. The King considered the founder members of the Royal Academy as very much *his* artists, and it seems likely that Paul and Thomas ranked among these because of their connection with the new Duke of Cumberland.

It was also in 1768 that Paul Sandby was appointed chief drawing master at the Royal Military Academy at Woolwich, at a salary of £150 per annum. This post, which he retained until his retirement in 1797, was the only official office that he held other than his early appointment as a military draughtsman. Most of the records of the RMA were destroyed in a fire in 1873, but the published extracts from the surviving records do include the following reference to Sandby's practice as 1st Drawing Master, as detailed in 1792 in a description of the 'course of studies which a Gentleman Cadet is to go through, before he is reported fit for a public examination for a Commission in the Royal Corps of Artillery and Engineers':

> Putting Perspective in Practice by Copying from Drawings, which qualifies them for Drawing from nature; teaches them the effect of Light and Shade; and makes them acquainted also with Aerial Perspective. Then to proceed to take views about Woolwich and other places; which teaches them at the same time to break ground, and forms the eye to the knowledge of it.[4]

In his work at Woolwich Paul Sandby was able to introduce a wide range of the sons of the aristocracy, gentry and lesser classes to the practice and appreciation of landscape drawing, and this certainly was a factor in the growing popularity of the collecting and practice of that aspect of British art. Paul Sandby also had other private pupils throughout his career, but here again we know very little detail, though it seems probable that some of his patrons, such as the Hon. Charles Greville and Sir Watkin Williams Wynn, were also his pupils. The latter is seen seated at the foot of a tree and sketching in a small study at Windsor,[5] and several other Paul Sandby figure drawings show young ladies drawing, among them the exquisite *A lady painting*, also at Windsor (fig. 8).[6]

Though, as has already been suggested, it seems likely that much of Paul Sandby's exhibited work in the 1760s was in oils, it is also probable that his great series of watercolour and bodycolour drawings of Windsor Castle and its surroundings belongs to the same decade. Thomas Sandby finally settled at Windsor in 1765, and Paul and his family (he was married in 1757 and his first child was born in 1767) will have stayed there regularly from then on, for the brothers and their families remained very close, as is shown by the fact that Paul's second son was christened Thomas Paul, and later married his uncle's second surviving daughter, Harriot, in 1786. Among the best-known works of Paul Sandby are his numerous drawings of Windsor Castle and its surroundings, of which an outstanding series, which is still being added to, is in the Royal Collection. Not one of these drawings is specifically dated, but Paul Oppé has suggested the years between 1760 and 1771 as the period of Paul Sandby's principal activity around Windsor Castle.[7] It seems probable that the beginning of this period should be brought forward by a few years. An impressive watercolour

FIG. 8 Paul Sandby, *A lady painting, c.* 1770. Pencil
and watercolour, $7\frac{5}{8} \times 6$. The Royal Library, Windsor; reproduced by gracious permission of Her Majesty The Queen

FIG. 9 Paul Sandby, *Windsor Castle: the Round Tower*,
?1756. Watercolour over pencil, $11\frac{1}{2} \times 20\frac{1}{2}$. The Provost and Fellows, Eton College

bequeathed to Eton College in 1948 – *Windsor Castle: the Round Tower* (fig. 9)[8] – bears the date 1756 on the sundial beneath a chimney in the centre of the building. That date is more likely to refer to the execution of this drawing than to the erection of a sundial, for it falls well within a period of neglect of the Castle, referred to by Sir Owen Morshead as 'the Dark Ages as far as Windsor is concerned'.[9] The Eton drawing is of the same high quality as some of those at Windsor which were formerly in the collection of Sir Joseph Banks, as for instance Nos. 24 and 25 in the Oppé catalogue, and may be taken as evidence for a slightly earlier start of Paul Sandby's work at Windsor.

Fortunately No. **9** in the present collection is a fine example of these Windsor drawings formerly in the Banks Collection, and it is interesting to note that there is a tradition identifying the two figures resting below a tree on the right of this broad composition as the brothers Thomas and Paul. Some of Paul's Windsor compositions exist in numerous versions, such as the series of views of the North Terrace (e.g. **10, 14** and **34**), and he must, presumably, have had a steady demand for these views, though there is no evidence of any actual royal patronage for them. However, it has been suggested that Paul Sandby was encouraged in his work at Windsor by George Brudenell, Duke of Montagu, who was Constable and Governor of the Castle from 1752 until his death in 1790. A superb set of Windsor views which belonged to the Duke are now at Drumlanrig, and Sandby's 1776 Windsor aquatints were dedicated to the Duke. Sandby exhibited a Windsor subject for the first time at the Society of Artists in 1763, and did so again each year from 1765 to 1768. Windsor subjects reappear at the Royal Academy in 1774 and 1775, and at intervals in later years. An exhibition confined to Paul Sandby's views of Windsor would show the artist at his very best, and might include one or two oil paintings, such as the pair of large canvases of the North Terrace in the Royal Collection and in Philadelphia.[10] Among the earliest drawings in such a Windsor exhibition there would be a group of figure drawings, including such striking examples as the interiors drawn at Sandpit Gate in about 1754.[11]

Two events that occurred soon after his appointment as Deputy Ranger in 1765 enabled Thomas Sandby to play a more active role in the improvement of the Great Park, with which the new Duke of Cumberland was as much concerned as his uncle had been. In 1768 a great flood destroyed much of the first Duke's work, particularly at Virginia Water, and in 1769

Henry Flitcroft, the architect in charge of much of this work, died. It seems clear that from now on Thomas Sandby was directly involved with the further development and improvement of the Great Park, and the numerous drawings connected with this work must date from the 1770s or later. It was only after a second, and equally destructive, flood in 1782, that the formation of Virginia Water was completed; by then George III had himself begun to take a personal interest in the Park and Forest, and he took over the Rangership on the death of his brother, Henry Frederick, in 1790. The King had already decided to make Windsor Castle his main country retreat in about 1776, and considerable alterations and extensions were begun in various parts of the Castle at that time. Thomas Sandby's only known involvement in these was his design of the architectural framework in St George's Chapel for Benjamin West's altarpiece in 1782.

As we have seen, the 1760s were a fruitful decade for Paul Sandby both from the point of view of preferment and status and from that of the paintings and drawings that he was producing. It was also, of course, this decade which saw the death of such leading artists as Hogarth and Lambert, and the rise to pre-eminence of Gainsborough, Reynolds and Richard Wilson, with all of whom Paul Sandby was in close contact in the moves resulting in the foundation of the Royal Academy in 1768. If Frederick, Prince of Wales, had not died prematurely in 1751, the London Art world would probably have achieved at an earlier date the cohesion and sense of purpose which the Academy finally gave it.

In 1769 Paul Sandby showed four works at the first RA Summer Exhibition, for which he was a member of the hanging committee, and Thomas showed two architectural designs. From then on the elder brother exhibited each year until 1773, and after that on only two more occasions, in 1781 and 1782. Paul, on the other hand, showed between one and nine works at all but four exhibitions until the year of his death in 1809. Some of his exhibits were described as watercolours and stained drawings in the catalogues, but it is impossible to be certain of the media of the others, though we can be confident that there were oil paintings and bodycolour drawings among them, particularly in the early and later years. In 1777 Paul exhibited two *Views near Naples* in aquatint, a new medium, which, as we shall see, he had used for the first time two years earlier. In the V & A collection there are a number of drawings by Paul (**11, 24** and **33**), and one by Thomas (**44**), that were included in Royal Academy exhibitions. These and drawings in other collections known to have been shown at the RA make it clear that watercolours submitted to the exhibitions were usually on an ambitious scale, and the same is, of course, true of the few known exhibited oil paintings and gouaches.

Paul Sandby's work in gouache or bodycolour is reasonably well represented in the V & A collection. There are two early examples, the highly detailed figure composition of *The removal from the Thames ... of the hulk which became the Chinese Junk on Virginia Water* (**2**), which dates from about 1755, and the *Classical landscape* (**5**), which is typical of his work in this medium in the 1760s. Here Paul was working in a tradition that was widespread throughout Europe, and in which he certainly proved himself a master. Dr Johnson Ball has suggested that Sandby may have been introduced to the medium as a boy in Nottingham, where members of the Dutch Verelst family of artists lived and worked for many years, and included portraits and flower paintings in bodycolour among their productions.[12] While that suggestion is largely speculative, it is certain that Paul Sandby was influenced by the work of Marco Ricci (1676-1730), the leading Italian artist using bodycolours for the depiction of landscape. That influence is very evident in the *Classical landscape* and also in the fine example in the Castle Museum at Nottingham, *Winchester Tower and part of the Hundred Steps* (fig. 10), which is in bodycolours on leather. Leather was commonly used by Marco Ricci, as in the series of over thirty such works by him acquired by George III from Consul Smith in about 1762, and still in the Royal Collection (fig. 11).[13] It seems likely that here Sandby was following the example of Marco Ricci, whom he is known to have admired and whose work he himself collected, in using leather for this Windsor subject, which is closely related to the much smaller watercolour of the same scene in the Royal Collection.[14]

It should be emphasized that Paul Sandby used bodycolours throughout his long career, as is illustrated by the other examples in this collection. The beautiful *Windsor Castle: the North Terrace looking west, at sunset* (**10**), which dates from about 1770, shows the artist at the height of his powers, and acts as a reminder that bodycolour was used partially or wholly in a considerable number of Sandby's Windsor drawings. No. **10**, with its vivid sunset, is one of the most 'romantic' of these, and in his later years Sandby used bodycolours most frequently in his more imaginative subjects, such as *An ancient beech tree* (**25**), which is dated 1794. This powerful composition is

FIG. 10 Paul Sandby, *Windsor Castle: Winchester Tower and Part of the Hundred Steps*, c. 1760. Bodycolour on leather, $18\frac{5}{8} \times 22\frac{1}{2}$. Castle Museum, Nottingham. Compare FIG. 11

FIG. 11 Marco Ricci (1676–1730), *The Courtyard of a
Country House*. Tempera on leather, 12¼ × 18. Windsor
Castle; reproduced by gracious permission of Her
Majesty The Queen. Compare FIG. 10

on a par with the even more Rubensian *The Rainbow* at Nottingham, and with several other major works in which a massive gnarled tree is the central feature. It seems likely that such ambitious compositions were intended for exhibition, and it is tempting to associate No. **25** with the pair entitled *Evening* and *Morning* that Paul Sandby showed at the RA in 1795 (Nos. 575 and 579), but there is no positive evidence for this.

It will have been noticed that there is a gap of some twenty years between Nos. **10** and **25**, and during these two decades, the 1770s and 1780s, Paul Sandby was working principally in watercolours and aquatint. However, it seems appropriate to continue the survey of the artist's work in bodycolours at this point. It has to be admitted that much of this later work is of a quality inferior to that of the examples already discussed. There are, for instance, great weaknesses, particularly in the drawing of the buildings and the animals, in the *View of the Keeper's Lodge, Easton Park, Suffolk* (**26**), which dates from the 1790s and which is typical of Paul Sandby's rather feeble manner at that time. When this manner is combined with the artist's more imaginative vision, as in *Dragoons galloping along the road at Vanbrugh Fields, Greenwich* (**28**), the result is more effective despite the stiffness of the figures. It is again the figures that are particularly weak in the contemporary *View in Windsor Forest* (**29**). Both these drawings bear inscriptions on the back referring to Ann Cobbe, and it is possible that she was a pupil of Sandby's at that time, and may have had a hand in their execution. However, even if this were so in the case of these two examples, the same weakness are repeated in other late bodycolour drawings for which there is no evidence of the participation of a pupil.

As is pointed out in the relevant catalogue entry, No. **34**, *Windsor Castle: the North Terrace looking west, at sunset*, provides striking evidence of the deterioration in the quality of Sandby's gouaches in the intervening decades when it is compared with No. **10**, the first-rate version of the same view dating from about 1770. However, something of the old quality is retained in the two final bodycolour drawings at the V & A, *The Old Welsh Bridge, Shrewsbury* (**35**) and *Carreg-Cennen Castle, Carmarthenshire* (**37**), which are both dated to about 1800. The picturesque old bridge at Shrewsbury was a favourite subject of Sandby's, of which at least twelve views by him are known today, most of them on the same ambitious scale as the present example. This is executed on canvas, and is an effective composition with high qualities of light and shade. Once again this large drawing is likely to have been a work intended for exhibition, and it is tempting to associate it with the two views of the Welsh Bridge which Sandby exhibited at the RA in 1801. *Carreg-Cennen Castle* is a much smaller work, but it, too, recaptures some of the quality found in Sandby's earlier work in bodycolours.

Notes

1. See Bruce Robertson in *Turner Studies*, Vol. 4(1984), pp. 44–6.
2. For the whole letter see Mary Woodall, *The Letters of Thomas Gainsborough*, 1963, pp. 87–91.
3. Robertson, 1985, No. 76.
4. *Records of the Royal Military Academy, 1741–1892*, 1893, p. 33.
5. Oppé, 1947, No. 371.
6. Oppé, 1947, No. 259.
7. Oppé, 1947, p. 8.
8. This drawing was bequeathed to Eton College in 1948 by Miss F. A. C. M.

Biddulph, who had herself inherited it from the Revd Hugh Pearson, Canon of Windsor.
9. Sir Owen Morshead, *Windsor Castle*, 1971, p. 68.
10. Sir Oliver Millar, *The Later Georgian Pictures in the Collection of Her Majesty The Queen*, 1969, No. 1055.
11. Oppé, 1947, Nos. 245–6 and 248–50.
12. See Ball, 1985, Chap. 9.
13. Sir Michael Levey, *The Later Italian Pictures in the Collection of Her Majesty The Queen*, 1964, Nos. 591–622.
14. Oppé, 1947, No. 50.

III Years of consolidation 1770–80

Four of Paul Sandby's seven 1770 RA exhibits were specifically described as watercolours in the catalogue, as were *all* his exhibits in the next three years. These facts may be taken as an indication that at this time Sandby was concentrating more and more on producing work in watercolours, the medium with which his name is principally associated. That supposition is strengthened by the fact that only two or three of the works he exhibited at the Society of Artists between 1760 and 1768 were designated as watercolours. This is not to say that Paul Sandby was not using the medium in his earlier years, for there are many watercolours of landscape and of figure subjects dating from the years in Scotland, and from the following two decades. It does, however, seem likely that most of these were studies either to record particular places or figures, or to assist in the composition of works in other media and of engravings. There are many such watercolour figure studies in the Carr Album (**52**) as well as the more mature and accomplished study of *The three daughters of the 2nd Earl of Waldegrave with Miss Keppel and a governess* (**6**), which dates from about 1770 or a little earlier. However, there are no early watercolour studies of landscape in this collection, in which the first notable watercolour landscape is the fine *Eton College and Windsor from the Playing Fields* (**9**), which dates from about 1770 and thus belongs to the period in which Sandby was using the medium for finished and exhibition drawings, to which category it certainly belongs.

The V & A collection includes several examples typical of Paul Sandby's work in watercolour in the 1770s. The harmonious view of *Hubberstone Priory, near Milford Haven* (**13**), which dates from about 1775, was engraved for *The Virtuosi's Museum* in 1778, as was the rather more precise and relatively toneless view of *Llandaff Cathedral* (**15**). Of about the same date as these two, and actually dated *1775*, is the rather weaker view of *Chepstow Castle* (**12**), which was engraved in aquatint in that year. The inscription on the back of this drawing records that Sandby 'retouched' it in 1788, and this and the present poor condition of the drawing may account for its rather disappointing quality. Also dated *1775*, and much larger and more ambitious than any of the watercolours discussed so far, is *Caesar's Tower and part of Warwick Castle, from the Island* (**11**), which was probably exhibited at the Royal Academy in 1775, and which was the basis of plate three of Sandby's series of four aquatints of Warwick Castle, published in 1775/6. Sandby's draughtsmanship is seen at its best in every element of this

FIG. 12 Thomas Sandby, *Study of Trees*, *c.* 1755. Pen and grey ink over pencil, with watercolour, on laid paper, $9\frac{1}{2} \times 11\frac{1}{2}$. Messrs. Sotheby's

impressive composition, which, though now rather faded, must rank as one of the outstanding examples of his work in watercolours in the present collection. The same quality is to be found in *Village street, Old Charlton, Kent* (**16**), which is dated to the later 1770s. This too is somewhat marred by its poor condition, but despite this it illustrates Sandby's drawing of buildings at its best. The complex roof structure and chimneys of the cottages are depicted with great detail, and the effect is enhanced by the skilful play of light and shade. In this composition, as in the view of Warwick Castle, Paul Sandby's figure drawing is also seen at its most effective, and all the men, women, children and dogs seem to be alive in, and belong to, the setting in which they are shown.

The high quality of Thomas Sandby's early watercolours has been referred to above, and is represented in the V & A in the fine view of *Windsor Castle from the Great Park* (**38**), which probably dates from the early 1750s. In this sheet the free and fluent drawing of the trees is characteristic, and these qualities are retained in later watercolours attributed to Thomas. A volume of drawings formerly in the collection of Paul Sandby and recently sold at Sotheby's[1] includes a small group of delicate watercolour studies of trees which are initialled *T.S.* in pencil and which are certainly by Thomas (fig. 12). These lively sketches, presumably drawn on the spot, support the attribution to Thomas of several drawings at Windsor and elsewhere, such as the *Windsor from the Lodge Grounds in the Great Park*[2] which is currently attributed to either Paul or Thomas. There are a considerable number of watercolour landscapes, of scenes in Windsor and elsewhere, for which a definite attribution to one or other of the brothers is difficult, but the high and pioneering quality of Thomas's early watercolours in the Netherlands, Scotland and Windsor does lend weight to the supposition that the architect brother is likely in later years to have continued his competent work in watercolours in landscape as well as in architectural and topographical drawings.

There has long been doubt as to which brother was responsible for the important pair of perspective views from the gardens of Somerset House in the Crowle Bequest at the British Museum.[3] Laurence Binyon attributed them to Thomas, but recently they have been re-attributed to Paul, to whom they had been attributed by J. T. Smith, Keeper of Prints at the British Museum from 1816 to 1833, who knew both brothers. However, the very architectonic drawing of the buildings and the specific characteristics of the drawing of the trees suggest to the present writer that Thomas is most likely to have been the author of these and similar drawings, though Paul will probably have inserted the figures, as he certainly did in other London scenes by his brother. If this attribution is accepted, then it lends support to the suggestion that Paul in fact made no finished watercolour drawings of major buildings or views in central London, though there are many such by his brother. Paul's depiction of London is almost wholly confined to the suburbs – Bayswater, Paddington and Greenwich, for instance – as we shall see when his watercolours of the 1780s are discussed.

Unfortunately there are no actual London views by Thomas in the V & A, but the *Design for the elevation of a prison* (**43**) may have been a proposal for a new London building. This and the more elaborate *Design for a National Mausoleum or Temple of Fame* (**42**) show Thomas Sandby's powers of design and draughtsmanship at their best. Such ambitious drawings may well have been executed as illustrations for his lectures as Professor of Architecture at the Royal Academy. He delivered six of these each year from 1770 onwards, though they were read for him when he was ill in the last two years of his life. It was the sixth lecture of each series that was illustrated by some forty designs, including, from about 1780 onwards, some of his well-known drawings of the 'Bridge of Magnificence', of which there are three in the present collection (**45-47**). It has always been supposed that the 'Bridge of Magnificence' drawings were used to illustrate the lectures from the beginning, but the close connection of Thomas Sandby's design with William Chambers's plans for the new Somerset House substantiates the suggestion that they cannot be earlier than about 1780, for the reconstruction of Somerset House did not begin until 1776, and in several of the drawings (including **47**) the river front is shown almost complete. The Sandby brothers were on very friendly terms with Sir William Chambers, and Thomas was probably familiar with his drawings for Somerset House. Even if the dating of about 1780 is accepted, Thomas would have had to have had access to Chambers's designs.

Additional support for the later dating of the 'Bridge of Magnificence' drawings is given by the fact that it was only in 1781 that Thomas exhibited two of them at the RA, where his final exhibit, in 1782, was the sadly faded and damaged *Strawberry Hill: Interior of the Gallery* (**44**), on which we know he began working some years earlier, as is fully discussed in the catalogue entry. Thus this complex drawing can also be taken as an example of Thomas Sandby's precise draughtsmanship in the 1770s. His work of this decade is further represented in a number of small drawings in the Carr Album: most notable among these are the two pen-and-ink drawings of architectural details associated with Sandby's design of the Freemasons' Hall (**52w** and **x**). Built in 1775 and 1776, and demolished in 1932, this fine classical building was Thomas Sandby's most important executed work, and his only major building in London. It was much admired at the time, and appears to have been a building which was on a par with the imaginative and informed qualities of Sandby's best architectural drawings. Though it seems that most of Thomas's life and work was now centred on Windsor, his membership of the Royal Academy and the Freemasons, and his lectures as Professor of Architecture, which continued to be well received and influential, assured his place at the centre of affairs in London in the 1770s. Thomas also continued to enjoy Royal patronage, for in April 1777 he was appointed Architect of the King's Works, in succession to Sir Robert Taylor, and in November 1780 he became Master Carpenter in the Office of Works. Nothing is known about his activities in these offices, and the latter was, in fact, abolished only two years after his appointment.

Some measure of Paul's continued success in this decade may be found in the fact that in 1772 he moved to the house at 4 St George's Row, Bayswater, which remained his home for the rest of his life. This appears to have been a substantial house, and it seems probable that the fine neoclassical studio behind it was erected by Paul – perhaps designed by his brother? (fig. 13). The house, which was later known as 23 Hyde Park Place and was demolished in 1901, had fine views over Hyde Park and was close to Bayswater Turnpike on the Oxford Road. We learn from the *Life* of the brothers' architect friend, James Gandon, that:

Sandby's vast store of knowledge in the Fine Arts, added to his high professional character, and the conversational powers which he possessed, drew round him a circle of intellectual and attached friends, comprising the most distinguished artists and amateurs of the day. His house became quite the centre of attraction, particularly during the spring and summer months, when, on each Sunday, after Divine Service, his friends assembled, and formed a conversazione on the arts, the sciences, and the general literature of the day.

Some of the eminent men and women that he met there are listed by Gandon – Charles Greville, William Mason and the Russian Princess

FIG. 13 Paul Sandby, *The artist's studio, St. George's Row, Bayswater, c.* 1775. Watercolour and body-colour on grey paper, 9 × 11. The Trustees of the British Museum, London. Compare **52k-m**

Dashkoff among them – and reference is made to the presence of 'almost every artist of eminence of that day'.[4]

Princess Dashkoff and the Hon. Charles Greville, younger son of Francis, 8th Baron Brooke and 1st Earl of Warwick, were pupils of Paul Sandby and are both cited as being involved in what was certainly the most important innovation of his artistic career in the 1770s, the 'discovery' and use of the aquatint method of engraving. Until recently Sandby was thought to have introduced this effective new technique, which was first developed by the French artist Jean Baptiste Le Prince in the late 1760s, into England. However, it was in fact Peter Burdett of Liverpool who can claim that distinction; his first aquatint is dated 1771, and was exhibited in the following year at the Society of Artists. It is now commonly accepted that Charles Greville purchased the formula of the aquatint process from Burdett and presented it to his master. However, Dr Ball has pointed out that the Russian Princess was almost certainly a pupil of Le Prince, either while the French artist was in Russia from 1758 to 1764 or while she herself was in Paris before coming to England, and that it may have been through her that Sandby gained his knowledge of Le Prince's aquatint method.[5]

Whatever the way in which Paul Sandby acquired his skill in aquatint, he was certainly the first British artist to use the new process extensively, to name it and to popularize it. His delight and excitement at mastering the new technique is reflected in two letters to his Edinburgh pupil, John Clerk of Eldin, preserved in the library at the Victoria and Albert Museum.[6] He wrote to him on 8 September 1775:

> I perceive you have been trying at Le Prince's Secret, know my good Friend I got a key to it and am perfect master of it, you will perceive by the inclosed first trials of mine I soon made a progress in it – I have already done 24 views in Wales and 4 Large Warwicks which I will send you as soon as they are published, I own no hobby horse in the world would suit me equal to this, indeed I have rid so closely these four months past I have scarcely done anything else, the work is so delightful and easy to me now in the execution I do it with the same ease but with more pleasure on paper . . .

The first twelve of the '24 views in Wales' were published in September 1775, with the following wording on the Frontispiece: 'XII Views in Aqua-tinta from Drawings Taken on the Spot in South-Wales Dedicated to the Honourable Charles Greville and Joseph Banks Esquire by Their Ever Grateful and Much Obliged Servant Paul Sandby. R.A.'. Plate 1 is a view

FIG. 14 Paul Sandby, *Chepstow Castle in Monmouthshire*, 1775. Aquatint, $9\frac{3}{8} \times 12\frac{3}{8}$. V & A (E. 267-1901). Compare **12**

of Chepstow Castle (fig. 14), for which the drawing is in the present collection (**12**). The material for this was assembled by Paul Sandby on a
seven-week tour undertaken from 25 June to 16 August 1773, in the com-
pany of Joseph Banks, John Lightfoot, and Dr Daniel Solander, all of
whom were intent on botanical rather than topographical interests. This
extensive tour and the resulting aquatints are fully described by Peter
Hughes in an article published in *The Burlington Magazine* in 1975.[7] Three
years earlier and in the same magazine the same author had published his
equally informative article on 'Paul Sandby and Sir Watkin Williams-
Wynn',[8] in which the artist's 1771 tour in North Wales is discussed. Having
been at Wynnstay in 1770 at the celebrations for the baronet's twenty-first
birthday, during which he painted some stage scenery, Sandby was there
again in the following August and spent some two weeks touring with Sir
Watkin in North Wales. It was during that tour that the artist collected
the material which became the basis of the second Welsh aquatint series,
XII Views in North Wales, which was not published until 1776.

Between the two sets of Welsh aquatints, which were, of course, the '24
views in Wales' referred to in the letter to John Clerk, Paul Sandby published the '4 Large Warwicks' also mentioned. These impressive plates are
considerably larger than the Welsh ones, and, as is seen in the *Part of
Warwick Castle from the S.E.* reproduced here (fig. 15), are more ambitious
in composition and execution than the first Welsh series and on a par with
the strikingly successful prints of the second Welsh series, which achieve a
memorable impression of some of the finest features of the Welsh landscape
and concentrate less on subjects of antiquarian interest than the earlier set
had done. The new aquatint method, with its fine tonal qualities, clearly
suited Sandby's manner at this time and gave great impetus to his development as a landscape rather than a topographical artist. Sandby was to
undertake two more series of Welsh subjects, *XII Views in Wales* published
in September 1777, and *XII Views in North and South Wales* published in
1786. This was his final series of prints in aquatint, and he was to produce
only one or two more individual plates. In all he was responsible for over
a hundred prints in that medium, the majority of them after his own
designs, and it should be remembered that Sandby's work in aquatint
during the 1770s and 1780s coincided with his major achievements in
watercolour, a medium most effectively reproduced by the aquatint engraving.

FIG. 15 Paul Sandby, *Part of Warwick Castle from the S.E.*, 1775/6. Aquatint, 12¾ × 18⅝. V & A (E. 902–1977). Compare **11**

In his depiction of Wales in the mid-1770s Paul Sandby was breaking new ground not only from the point of view of technique but also – and equally important in the study of British landscape art – of subject matter. It seems likely that the scenery in Sandby's 1761 *Welsh Bard* canvas was imaginary, and though Richard Wilson produced some of his great Welsh canvases in the mid-1760s, William Woollett's highly successful engraving of his *Snowdon from Llyn Nantlle* was not published by Boydell until 1775. Thomas Pennant's famous *Tour in Wales* was only published in 1778, and William Gilpin's Wye tour pictures, though carried out in 1770, were not published until 1782. Thus Sandby's travels in Wales and the resulting prints were well ahead of fashion, as was, of course, Sir Watkin Williams-Wynn when he invited the artist to accompany him in 1771. The wild and romantic Welsh scenery that Paul Sandby visited on that occasion must have reminded him of what he had seen when in the Highlands in the 1740s, but that scenery was not to attract artists and travellers in search of landscape until the turn of the century.

Though so much engaged with his own work in aquatint at this time, Sandby continued to produce drawings for engraving in copper, and indeed publication of the major series of landscape and topographical engravings after him began in February 1778 and was completed in January 1781. Entitled *The Virtuosi's Museum*, this series consisted of 108 plates of 'Select Views in England, Scotland and Ireland, Drawn by P. Sandby, Esq. R.A.', and was published in separate numbers, each containing three engravings with accompanying text, by George Kearsley, for whose *Copperplate Magazine* Sandby had produced many views in the previous four years. In 1783, 42 of the *Copperplate Magazine* plates were added to those of *The Virtuosi's Museum* and reissued by John Boydell as *A Collection of One Hundred and Fifty Select Views in England, Wales, Scotland and Ireland*, with texts in both English and French. Many of the leading engravers of the day were employed to copy Sandby's drawings, among them James Fittler, M. A. Rooker, T. Mazel and W. Watts. Two watercolours engraved for this series are in the V & A (**13** and **15**), and the engraving after one of them, *Hubberstone Priory*, is reproduced here (fig. 16).

In this aspect of his work Paul Sandby was again in the van of fashion and taste, as is indicated by the following passage from the Preface to *The Virtuosi's Museum*:

> In the choice of our subjects ... we follow an illustrious example. The renowned Empress of Russia ... has paid the highest compliment to the genius and taste of this country; by procuring, at an immense expence, views of all the noblemen and gentlemen's seats, and of every delightful spot throughout the kingdom, drawn on the spot, and painted upon setts of china dishes and plates. If these views appear so enchanting in the eyes of this Princess, surely it must afford the highest satisfaction to Britons themselves, to have in their possession complete representations of them on a better plan for preservation, and on much easier terms.

Here the author is referring to the vast cream-ware dinner and desert service of some 1300 pieces which Catherine the Great commissioned from Josiah Wedgwood in 1773, on each piece of which was to be painted a different view representing 'British scenery', including one or two after drawings by Paul Sandby. The completed service was exhibited in London in June and July 1774, and this enterprising undertaking has rightly been considered as an important element in the progress of British topographical drawing, which greatly enhanced the demand for such work at the very time when Paul Sandby was probably the best-known artist working in this area.

It should be remembered that during the 1770s both Gainsborough and Wilson were unable to find a steady sale for their landscape paintings. The former was forced to continue his work as a portrait painter in order to make a living, while in 1776 Wilson was glad to accept the office of Librarian at the Royal Academy as a much needed source of additional income. It was during these years that Paul Sandby secretly bought drawings and paintings by Wilson and encouraged others to do likewise. Samuel Scott had retired from London in 1765, though on the other hand P.J. de Loutherbourg (1740–1812) chose to settle in the capital in 1771, after early success in Paris, where he had been elected a member of the Académie in 1766. He showed profusely at the Royal Academy throughout the 1770s, but was not elected ARA until 1780, and then RA in the following year. The majority of his exhibits, both paintings and drawings, were landscapes, but most of these revealed his effortless eclecticism rather than a personal style. There were other landscape artists painting and exhibiting at this time, for instance George Barret, William Marlow, and Michael Angelo Rooker, but they tended to remain in the background rather than the forefront of the artistic scene. In this atmosphere of lack of recognition and of material difficulties among landscape artists, Paul Sandby's considerable success in the 1770s becomes all the more remarkable, and it is not surprising that he was not able to maintain this record in the following decade.

NOTES

1. Sotheby's, 11 July 1985, lot 10.
2. R.L. 17751.
3. L.B. 8 & 9; Lindsay Stainton, 1985, Nos. 21 a & b.
4. Gandon, pp. 39–40.
5. Ball, 1985, pp. 217–24.
6. V & A Library 13466 (MSS PP 75–6).
7. 'Paul Sandby's Tour of Wales with Joseph Banks', *Burlington Magazine*, CXVII (1975), pp. 452–7.
8. 'Paul Sandby and Sir Watkin Williams-Wynn', *Burlington Magazine*, CXIV (1972), pp. 459–66.

FIG. 16 T. Mazel after Paul Sandby, *Hubberstone
Priory, Pembrokeshire*, 1778. Copper engraving, $5\frac{1}{8} \times 7\frac{1}{8}$.
V & A Library. Compare **13**

IV   Later years 1780-96

In 1780 Thomas Sandby reached the age of 57 and Paul of 49, and both were at the height of their powers and careers. In that year the Royal Academy moved into its new Rooms in Somerset House. At the opening, on 16 October, the President, Sir Joshua Reynolds, delivered a short address – his *Ninth Discourse* – and expressed his satisfaction at 'seeing the Arts in a state to which they never arrived before in this nation'. Politically this was a period of unrest, which came to a head in June with the anti-papist Gordon Riots, during which the mob, led by Lord George Gordon, held London for a week. Order was only restored when the troops were called in, and Paul Sandby made numerous studies of the military en-campments in Hyde Park and elsewhere which continued until August, and were apparently considered an attractive new source of entertainment by many Londoners. In 1781 he exhibited six views of the various encamp-ments, and he also issued four large and two sets of small aquatints of these scenes. The Carr Album contains several small studies connected with these (**52 0**, etc.). In some of Sandby's Encampment drawings the draughtsman-ship is somewhat crude and free in detail, both in the rendering of figures and of trees and other landscape features.

This apparent decline in his artistic powers seems likely to have been the result of a deliberate change of style rather than of an unavoidable waning of ability, and may be associated with a conscious policy to produce land-scape rather than topography, for despite their weakness of detail many of the Encampment compositions retain a good overall effect. This later man-ner of Paul Sandby can be seen at its best in a drawing of about 1790 at Windsor, *The Serpentine River, Hyde Park* (fig. 17), which Paul Oppé tellingly described as 'effective when seen at a distance and of interest as showing the stage of development reached before Girtin or Constable in the appre-ciation of a commonplace scene without conventional, topographic or sen-timental appeal'.[1] There are a number of watercolours in the V & A illustrating this changed style of the 1780s and 90s. The change-over period can be seen in the pair depicting the Tea Gardens and the Public House in Bayswater (**17** and **18**) in which considerable freedom of detail is com-bined with an effective fluency in the rendering of light and shade. The same fluency of light and shade combined with a further lessening of detail is found in the three mountainous landscapes (**19, 20** and **22**) which are typical of many such 'picturesque' compositions of the 1780s. The Claude-like *The Round Temple* (**21**), which is dated 1788, unites the indivi-

FIG. 17 Paul Sandby, '*The Serpentine River, Hyde Park*', *c.* 1790. Pencil and watercolour, with body-colour highlights, 13½ × 21⅞. The Royal Library, Windsor; reproduced by gracious permission of Her Majesty The Queen

dual qualities of the two preceding pairs of drawings in a powerful and unified composition. Somewhat less satisfactory, especially in its very feeble figures, is the view of Rye House (**23**), in which Sandby has clearly found difficulty in combining the drawing's topographical purpose with his imaginative style.

However, there is no evidence of such difficulty in the much more ambitious exhibition drawing entitled '*Morning: View on the Road near Bayswater Turnpike*' (**24**), which is dated 1790 and was exhibited at the Royal Aca-

demy in the following year together with an 'Evening view near Bayswater', which is untraced today. In this important drawing the figures and
other staffage elements show Paul Sandby's draughtsmanship at it best,
and even in its present faded and dirty condition the drawing demonstrates
the artist's mastery of composition based on the subtle rendering of effects
of light and shade. There is something of the same quality in the *Scene in
Windsor Forest* (**27**), which belongs to the large number of Windsor Woodyard and similar scenes drawn by Sandby in the 1790s in the loose, late
style in which there is almost no outline. Some of these drawings, including
several at Windsor,[2] are dated 1792, and in the following year Sandby
exhibited two Windsor Woodyard scenes at the RA. He probably sketched
these scenes while staying with his brother, son and daughter-in-law, in
Windsor Great Park; at this time the informal rural features of the woodyard and its surroundings attracted him more than the buildings of the
Castle and its immediate rather formal surroundings. The earlier Windsor
Castle views were the work of Sandby the topographical artist, while the
later Woodyard scenes are by Sandby the landscape artist.

In the 1780s the elder brother, Thomas, also became increasingly interested and involved in landscape, for this was the period when he was at
last employed on the development of Virginia Water, begun by William,
Duke of Cumberland, and continued after his death in 1765 by his nephew
and successor as Ranger of Windsor Forest, Prince Henry Frederick, who
was in turn created Duke of Cumberland in 1766. The original architect
of the lake was almost certainly Henry Flitcroft, who died in 1769, and
may even still have been involved in making good the serious damage
caused by floods in 1768. Thomas Sandby's opportunity came after more
flood damage in 1782, after which he was responsible for the enlargement
of the lake and the building of a new cascade and grotto.[3] In the present
collection there are three watercolours connected with this work (**48-50**),
and there are further groups of such drawings in the collections at Windsor,
the Bodleian Library (Gough Collection) and elsewhere. These Virginia
Water designs are characterized by their loose drawing and their pale
colouring, and they are quite different in feeling and technique from
Thomas Sandby's earlier precise architectural drawings. It seems that in
the 1780s both brothers underwent a deliberate change of style and
adopted a freer and more fluid manner in their use of watercolours. This
loose style is also seen in Thomas's intriguing *Design for a gateway or bridge*

in imitation of Gothick ruins (**51**) and in a number of small studies in the Carr Album. Among these is a rapid pencil drawing (**52y**) connected with the building of the bleach works at Llewenny near Denbigh, which he designed in about 1785 for the Hon. Thomas Fitzmaurice. This was one of the architect's last-known commissions; the very last was probably the stone bridge over the Thames at Staines, which was built between 1792 and 1797, but failed in 1799 and was replaced by an iron bridge a few years later.

It seems that the brothers and their families always retained a close relationship, and in 1786 that relationship was strengthened even further by the marriage of Paul's second son, Thomas Paul, to Thomas's second surviving daughter, Harriot. The young couple lived with Thomas at Windsor, and were to have numerous children. Thomas's second wife, Elizabeth, had died in 1782. Thomas Paul had followed in his father's footsteps as an artist, and was to succeed him as Chief Drawing Master at the Royal Military Academy at Woolwich in 1796. Today just a handful of drawings which can be attributed to him with confidence are known, and he only exhibited twice at the Royal Academy, in 1791 and 1792. Thomas Paul's elder and only brother, Paul, chose a military career, but, despite his father's efforts on his behalf, failed to gain adequate promotion. He was still a lieutenant in the Royal Scotch Fusiliers when he died at Barbados on 1 August 1793, much to his father's grief.

Paul Sandby's interest in 'pure' landscape is reflected in one of his major commissions of the 1790s, the decoration in 1793 of the dining room at Drakelow Hall, near Burton-on-Trent in Derbyshire, for Sir Nigel Gresley, Bart. Working in distemper on plaster Sandby decorated all the walls of the room to emulate a clearing in a forest encircled by paling, and having at one end a view over a valley, which is very Welsh in feeling and possibly represents Dolbadern Castle in its fine setting on Llyn Peris, with Snowdon beyond. The colouring suggests autumn and the mood is one of harmonious tranquillity. The original room featured a chimneypiece simulating a grotto and made of real spars, ores and shells, and the ceiling was painted as an open sky. The painted room was about forty feet long, and the coved ceiling nearly twenty-two feet high. Drakelow Hall was dismantled and demolished in 1934, at which time the Victoria and Albert Museum purchased the wall with the view, which was restored and re-erected in the Costume Court, where it is still to be seen today (fig. 18). This unique

FIG. 18 Paul Sandby, End wall from the painted room at Drakelow Hall, Derbyshire, 1793. Distemper on plaster, height 22 ft. V & A (P. 12 – 1934)

room, which bore Paul Sandby's signature and the date *1793*, is said to have been painted in two months,[4] and the surviving wall shows that the artist was working with complete authority on this large scale, in a manner that is in some ways a cross between the style of his 1760s 'Marco Ricci' gouache drawings and the contemporary fluid watercolour technique discussed earlier in this chapter. How he acquired the skill to design and work on this scale is a puzzle, to which the theatrical work that Sandby executed at Wynnstay in 1770 may provide a clue. The only known precedent for such a painted landscape room is the drawing room decorated in about 1781 by George Barret for William Lock at Norbury Park in Surrey, and in its overall character Sandby's room is somewhat similar to Barret's, but there is no evidence of direct influence.

The Drakelow Hall commission must have been something of a shot in the arm for Paul Sandby, who had ceased to produce any more aquatints, presumably because they were not selling well enough, and who was also undertaking little work for the engravers in the 1790s. He continued to exhibit up to four works each year at the Royal Academy, and he was still active as a senior member of that body. He must also have been pleased by the favourable comments made in 1794 by Anthony Pasquin (John Williams) in his *A Liberal Critique of the Present Exhibition of the Royal Academy*: 'Mr Paul Sandby's drawings should be mentioned as exertions of the first order; they are cabinet gems of exquisite note'. However, there is little doubt that Paul Sandby's reputation and success were on the wane by 1796.

The elder brother was too ill that year to deliver his annual lectures, and they were read for him during the last two years of his life by his friend Edward Edwards, ARA, who had been elected the RA Professor of Perspective in 1788.

NOTES

1. Oppé, 1947, No. 185.
2. Oppé, 1947, Nos. 91–6.
3. This account of the work on Virginia Water is based on the Hon. Jane Roberts's

unpublished lecture, 'The Sandby Brothers at Windsor'.

4. See W. T. Whitley, *Art in England, 1800–1820*, 1930, p. 152.

V   The final years 1797–1809

When Anne Sandby, Paul's wife, died on 6 November 1797, her husband
was in his mid-sixties and her brother-in-law was nearly seventy-four years
old. Thomas had already been ill for some time and survived only a few
more months, dying at Windsor on 25 June 1798. On his own instructions
he was buried without pomp at Windsor, and a month after his death a
general assembly of the Royal Academy elected George Dance to fill his
place as Professor of Architecture, though it appears that he did not deliver
any lectures. Thomas Sandby remains a shadowy figure, both as regards
his work and his character. As will already have become clear, very little
of substance is known about the former, and unless new sources of information come to light he must remain one of the least-known of the more
eminent architects of his day. There are sufficient clues concerning
Thomas's character to indicate that he was a jovial and friendly man, an
affectionate husband and father, a loyal colleague and an attentive teacher.
Throughout his long life he retained the custom of composing verses
addressed to his friends, first seen in lines accompanying a drawing by Paul
sent as an invitation to Theodosius Forrest in February, 1753:

> Receive this humble Sketch and Scrawl
> From Poet Tom and Painter Paul
> Sent to inform you we at night
> Intend to deal in Shade and Light
> Or you may call it Light and Shade
> No matter which if both be made
> So you (like a good boy) prepare
> To sit or Sketch a figure here . . .[1]

A fair number of such verses survive, and from them one gains a sense
of Thomas's humour and good will. His keen powers of observation are
displayed in an unpublished Journal written in August 1774 during a *Tour
Through Part of Yorkshire and Derbyshire, performed by Messres. Thomas Sandby,
Capt: Robt. Elves, William Tyler, Theo: Forrest and Samuel Cotes*. The journal
takes the form of letters to his wife, and is accompanied by a number of
watercolour and pen and ink drawings, mostly of houses visited during the
tour. There are also two striking drawings of the famous caves at Castleton,
of which Thomas gives an especially lively account.[2]

Though he had ceased to engrave aquatints Paul Sandby continued to
produce numerous drawings in the later 1790s and probably up to the time
of his death. During these late years he returned to the use of bodycolours,
and, as we shall see, also to oils. On occasion he mixed the media of
watercolour and bodycolour, as, for example, in the *View in Windsor Forest*
(**29**), which is dated 1793, and the *View of Rochester, Kent* (**30**). In both

these compositions the figures are especially weak and wrong in scale, and it is tempting to account for such weaknesses by the participation of assistants or pupils. However, such an explanation can only be based on supposition, for there is no factual evidence to support it. On the other hand, it seems more than likely that the elderly artist, whom we know to have been constantly short of funds in his final years, would have welcomed help in producing drawings for sale. Further support for such ideas may be found in the variability in the quality of his late drawings, and in the presence of an artist son, who was himself failing to find a market for his own work.

The variable quality of Paul Sandby's late work in watercolours is well illustrated by a comparison between two drawings in the V & A, the bold and harmonious *Roadway through Windsor Forest* (**31**) and the somewhat weak and unimaginative view of *High Force, or Fall of the Tees, near Middleton High Tor* (**32**). The former, especially in its depiction of the gnarled and decaying tree, demonstrates Sandby's powers in composing a telling and romantic landscape; the latter entirely fails to convey the fact that its subject is considered to be one of the most impressive waterfalls in England. The weakness of such late watercolour drawings becomes all the more apparent when they are compared with some of the splendid exhibition pieces of the same years, most of which are in bodycolour or a mixture of bodycolour and watercolour. The V & A's *An ancient beech tree* (**25**) and *The Old Welsh Bridge, Shrewsbury* (**35**) are examples, and at the Fitzwilliam Museum there is a remarkable composition, which combines the main features of both these V & A pieces, entitled *A view of Old Shrewsbury Bridge,* (fig. 19). This deliberately imaginative and picturesque composition combining the carefully drawn 'realism' of a section of the bridge with the boldly rendered gnarled trunk of the ancient tree is completed by the inclusion in the foreground of a group of timeless figures which suggest the 'romantic world of hermits and peasants'.[3]

Dating from around 1800, this work and other equally impressive ones from the same period illustrate Paul Sandby's determination to remain among the innovators in British landscape art at the close of the eighteenth century. In the 1780s Gainsborough had produced his great romantic landscape compositions and fancy pictures, a lead followed by such artists as P. J. de Loutherbourg and Joseph Wright of Derby in the 1790s, at the end of which decade the young J. M. W. Turner began to exhibit canvases in

FIG. 19 Paul Sandby, *A view of Old Shrewsbury Bridge*, *c.* 1800. Bodycolour, watercolour and black
ink over traces of black chalk, $24\frac{1}{2} \times 18\frac{3}{8}$. Fitzwilliam Museum, Cambridge

FIG. 20 Paul Sandby, *Landscape with a lake*, 1808. Oil on canvas, $10\frac{1}{2} \times 18\frac{1}{2}$. Yale Center for British Art, Paul Mellon Collection

a related tradition. However, in the final years of his long career Paul Sandby began again to work in oils, as was reported in a letter dated 4 December 1806 from Thomas Paul Sandby to their Bristol friend, George Cumberland: 'My father is just come in from dining at Lord Maynard's ... The Old Gentleman (who is quite well) desires his best regards to you, he has taken to paint in oils and I think most happily'.[4] A few days later, on 13 January, Joseph Farington recorded in his *Diary* that Sandby 'had since August last been employed *in painting in oil*, and had finished a dozen pictures – He said the price of *glass* for drawings is now so high as to make it formidable, which had caused him to adopt a practice attended with less expense.'[5] A considerable number of these late oil paintings are known today, most of them on a small scale and somewhat loosely painted in pale colours. The *Landscape with a lake* reproduced here (fig. 20) is a typical example, which is dated 1808. In that year Paul Sandby exhibited 11 works at the recently formed British Institution, and judging by the dimensions given it is probable that these were all oil paintings on a slightly larger scale than *Landscape with a lake*. In the final paragraph of the Memoir of his father, T. P. Sandby wrote: 'Till within a few days of his death, he continued to paint, and during fourteen days only preceding that event, he finished his largest work in oil, which possesses equal spirit and truth, with any of his former productions in that way.'[6]

There is considerable evidence, among it Farington's report of the expense of glass for drawings, that in the closing years of his career Paul Sandby was having financial problems and that his drawings were not selling as well as they had done. Old age had presumably largely brought his touring days to an end, and an additional reason for the change from topographical to imaginary and romantic landscape subjects may well have been that he could no longer travel in order to record new subjects. However, he remained active in London and he seems to have been a frequent visitor to Englefield Green in Surrey, where Thomas Paul and his family had settled after Thomas's death.

In London much of his time was taken up with the affairs of the Royal Academy, as is indicated by quite frequent references to him by Joseph Farington in his *Diary*. Though Farington describes some of the business concluded at a meeting of the RA Council which he and Paul Sandby attended on 28 December 1799, and refers to a letter sent by the President, Benjamin West, who was indisposed (Farington had called on him earlier that day, and records a long discussion with him), he does not mention that that letter also reported that 'His Majesty had been Graciously pleased to nominate me [Sandby] to officiate for Mr Burch in the Library of the Royal Academy during his Indisposition'. We learn of this from two unpublished letters written to West by Sandby on 29 December thanking him profusely for having obtained this temporary appointment for him. The quotation above is from the formal letter; the accompanying personal letter Sandby begins as follows: 'I have to make my most grateful acknowledgement to you for the ever friendly endeavours to serve me, the communication you sent to the Councl last night, shows plainly notwithstanding your confinement at home by a severe fit of the gout, you found means to gain the request I made of you.'[7] We must presume that one reason behind Sandby's request for the temporary appointment of Librarian was the emolument connected with it. Thus in 1799 Sandby found financial relief in a Royal Academy office, as his friend Richard Wilson, who was elected Librarian in 1776, had done some twenty years earlier.

We gain some further knowledge of Sandby's state of health and of his character from the second paragraph of his personal letter to the President:

> A very severe Cold which still hangs on me besides offers sharp hints of a returning gout has prevented my paying you any respects for some time back, the necessity of my going to the Council last night to make up a sufficient number to enter on the business of the Academy [Farington records that only six members attended with Richard Cosway in the Chair], and notwithstanding my being shut up close in a Coach both there and back. I find to day I am worse for it, but will take the earliest opportunity that will allow me to pay my respects in person.

Benjamin West was eight years younger than his correspondent; one wonders, how much was Sandby writing 'with his tongue in cheek'?

Farington's *Diary* provides several more glimpses of Paul Sandby's activities at the RA in the closing years of his life. On 11 May 1806 he recorded a conversation with Benjamin West, during which the President said 'that Richards told him that When Sandby, as Deputy President, Yenn & He, Richards, went to the King to have the list of Election of Officers signed, His Majesty signed the papers but did not, as when Mr West went, enter into conversation'. Some 18 months later at the Academy Annual General Meeting on 10 December 1807 attended by twenty-seven Members, including Sandby, West was re-elected President, and three other Members who stood against him, Sandby, Beechey and Hoppner, received only one vote each, but Sandby and Beechey remained on the Council. J. M. W. Turner was elected Professor of Perspective at the same meeting, without opposition. He replaced the Sandbys' old friend Edward Edwards, who had died the previous year. Henry Tresham was elected to succeed John Opie as Professor of Painting, and Farington records that 'Fuseli left the room before the ballot'. At the close of the long day's business Farington 'shook hands with Sandby & had lively conversation with Him for the first time in many years', but the nature of the conversation is not mentioned. Sandby did not attend the last two General Meetings of 1807, but attended again on 10 February 1808, when two painters, Henry Howard and Thomas Phillips, were elected RA. Both of them were nearly forty years younger than Sandby, who was by then one of the very few surviving Founder Members.

Unfortunately Joseph Farington made only two very brief entries in his *Diary* in November 1809. The first, for 6 November, recorded the election as ARAs of David Wilkie and George Dawe; the second, written two days later, recorded the death of Paul Sandby – 'This day [he had actually died on the preceding day] died Paul Sandby R.A. at His House at St. George's Row, Oxford Turnpike, aged 84'. Farington was not the only one to be confused about Paul Sandby's age at this time – he was actually 78 when he died – for T. P. Sandby closed his Memoir of his father with the following words: 'at the conclusion of his eighty-fourth year, he left this world affectionately remembered and beloved by all who knew him'. That Paul Sandby was a friendly and amiable man is confirmed by his surviving portraits, and the following summing up of his father's character is certainly more reliable than T. P. Sandby's chronicling of his age.

Those early impressions [he wrote] formed by gentlemanly habits and feeling, which are never to be eradicated or mistaken, were very conspicuous in Mr. Sandby. There was a politeness and affability in his address, a sprightliness and vivacity in his conversation, together with a constant equanimity of temper, which joined with his having been the friend and companion of such men as Foote, Churchill, Garrick, Goldsmith, Macklin, and others of the same class, rendered his society and conversation singularly animating and interesting. Arrived at an age which few are permitted to attain, and spared almost all those infirmities which so generally accompany the accumulated years of man, his vigour of mind abated not to the last.[8]

However, it seems that Thomas Paul may also have been somewhat sanguine in his description of his father's state of health in his closing years, for, as is recorded by W. T. Whitley, in 1808 Paul was granted a pension of £60 a year by the Royal Academy in response to an appeal for assistance 'owing to advanced age and infirmities, and failure of employment'.[9] This occurrence confirms the suggestions made earlier in this chapter that in his final years Paul was struggling unsuccessfully to find a new market. Further confirmation of this can be found in Farington's terse comments in his *Diary* on 2 May 1811, recording his visit to the Christie's sale of Sandby's drawings: 'There was a large Collection of drawings by the late P. Sandby, & I could not but sensibly feel the great difference between His work & those of Artists who now practice in Water Colours. His drawings so divided in parts, so scattered in effect – detail prevailing over general effect.' In his final years the 'father of English watercolour' was at last out of fashion and behind the times, and it should be remembered that Paul Sandby was in no way involved with the foundation of the Society of Painters in Water Colours (now RWS) in 1804, and that he never exhibited with the Society. It is, indeed, worth noting that during the very years that the Society was being formed and held its first highly successful exhibition – 1803–5 – Paul Sandby did not show anything at the RA, and that in the following year he began to exhibit oils again. Whether all this was the result of ill-health or of disappointment by his omission from the new society is unlikely ever to be known.

NOTES

1. The drawing is in the Museum of London: see E. H. Ramsden, 'The Sandby Brothers in London', *Burlington Magazine*, LXXXVIII (1947), pp. 15–18.
2. The Journal is in the collection of Mr Sidney Sabin, to whom I am most grateful for telling me about it, and allowing me to study it and to refer to it.
3. See Peter Bicknell, *Beauty, Horror and Immensity*, Fitzwilliam Museum, Cambridge, 1981, No. 116.
4. B. L., Cumberland Papers 36500, fol. 427–8.
5. Farington *Diary*, Vol. VIII, p. 2944.
6. Oppé, *Burlington*, p. 147.
7. These two letters are in the Pierpont Morgan Library, New York.
8. Oppé, *Burlington*, p. 147.
9. W. T. Whitley, *Art in England, 1800–1820*, p. 139.

Catalogue **2**   Paul Sandby, *The removal from the Thames at the Bells of Ouseley of the hulk which became the Chinese Junk on Virginia Water*

Catalogue **4**   Paul Sandby, *The Old Bridge at Windsor*

Catalogue **6**   Paul Sandby, *The three daughters of the 2nd Earl of Waldegrave with Miss Keppel and a governess*

Catalogue **9**   Paul Sandby, *Eton College and Windsor from the Playing Fields*

Catalogue **11**   Paul Sandby, *Caesar's Tower and part of Warwick Castle, from the Island*

Catalogue **21**   Paul Sandby, *The Round Temple*

Catalogue **24**   Paul Sandby, *'Morning: View on
the Road near Bayswater Turnpike'*

Catalogue **25**   Paul Sandby, *An ancient beech tree*

Catalogue **37** Paul Sandby, *Carreg-Cennen
Castle, Carmarthenshire*

Catalogue **38**   Thomas Sandby, *Windsor Castle*
from the Great Park, near the end of the Long Walk

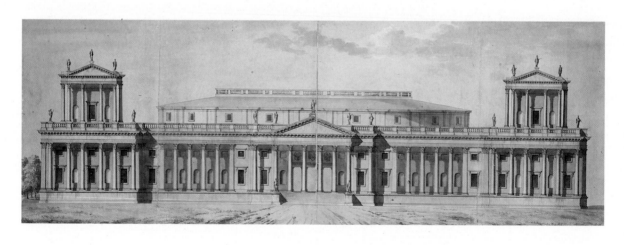

Catalogue **42**   Thomas Sandby, *Design for a*
National Mausoleum or Temple of Fame

VI Epilogue

It was presumably Thomas Sandby's brother and son-in-law who organized the sale of 'Drawings, Prints, Books, and Books of Prints, the Property of the Late Thomas Sandby, Esq.', which was held at Leigh and Sotheby in July, 1799. The sale took five days and comprised 400 lots. It included large numbers of drawings of various categories, including 27 lots described as 'Drawings by Mr Sandby, Used for his Lectures at the Royal Academy'. This wholesale dispersal of Thomas Sandby's sketches, drawings and plans, frequently divided into large lots, was certainly a major factor in the subsequent confusion in attributing work to him, especially as very few of the drawings known today are signed or inscribed by him.

Similar sales, on this occasion organized by Thomas Paul alone, followed the death of Paul Sandby, whose will had made his surviving son his sole heir. Before the first of these, which was held at Christie's on 2, 3 and 4 May 1811, he wrote several letters to his Bristol friend George Cumberland, indicating that he was having a difficult time sorting out the contents of his father's studio. In one such letter he stressed how busy he had been since his father's death 'in getting into something like an arrangement, the mass of papers he has left of every kind, and indeed it appears that, the more I sort them, the more I confuse myself, and them too'.[1] Before his own death, which occurred in 1832, Thomas Paul had arranged three further sales of his father's work, in 1812, 1817 and 1824, and one of his own, in 1827. It is probable that in all these sales the actual work of Paul Sandby was diluted by that of his numerous pupils and followers, among them his sons and his daughter. There was certainly also confusion with the work of his elder brother, Thomas, and indeed the catalogue of the 1799 sale of Thomas's works often fails to make it clear whether the drawings listed are by him or by Paul, and some definitely attributed to the latter were included in that sale.

The Paul Sandby sales also included his large and varied collections of paintings, drawings and prints by other artists of all schools. Most significant among these were his drawings by Richard Wilson and the large number of works by Marco Ricci. Typical of the confused way in which these sales were arranged are the first twelve (actually fourteen) lots of 'Drawings' offered on the second day of the 1812 sale, which was largely devoted to the artist's collections rather than to his own work:

1   A pair of drawings by Barrett
2   View of Whitby Abbey, Nicholson, and 1 more

3	Pair views, Horsleydown, &c. Cleveley
	Pair of views of Dover, Ditto
5	View on the Wye, by Wheatley
6	Four drawings by Girtin, &c.
7	Two pair of high-finished water colour drawings by Callender
8	Four views of Warwick castle, coloured by P. Sandby
9	Pair of high-finished views of Woolwich
*9	A beech tree in Luton Park, Sandby
**9	Five drawings, Guercino, &c.
10	Ditto ditto in water colours by Marco Ricci – *fine, on pannel*
11	A pair of ditto on ditto
12	Six Hindu drawings – *very fine*

From all this it will be seen that it is difficult, indeed almost impossible, to identify surviving Sandby drawings with specific lots in any of the Sandby sales. However, it is known that the collection of Sandby drawings in the Royal Library at Windsor owes its foundation to the purchases made on his behalf at the 1799 and 1811 sales by George IV when he was still Prince of Wales. The details of these purchases – they include 48 drawings in the 1811 sale – and of the formation of the Royal Collection are succinctly outlined by Paul Oppé in his 1947 catalogue. The next known major accessions for the Royal Collection were made at the sale at Christie's in 1876 of the great series of Paul Sandby's views of Windsor and Eton that had belonged to Sir Joseph Banks, one of his principal early patrons. Happily additions to the Sandby collections at Windsor have been made regularly since then and are still being made today.

Several of the Sandbys' descendants became collectors of their forebears' work, most notably William Arnold Sandby (*c.* 1828–1904), who was Thomas's great-grandson and the historian of the Royal Academy (two volumes published in 1862), and also the author of *Thomas and Paul Sandby – Royal Academicians*, published in 1892. W. A. Sandby was an avid collector of his forebears' work, and shortly before his death he assigned and bequeathed many examples from his Sandby collection to the British Museum, the V & A, the Castle Museum at Nottingham, and other museums and galleries all over the country. Though there are many very fine examples of the work of the brothers, especially Paul, among the W. A. Sandby donations, there are also many doubtful drawings, which indicate that W. A. Sandby was a somewhat uncritical collector. Unfortunately the fact that his widespread gifts and bequests included so many weak drawings has made it difficult to achieve a satisfactory standard of attribution.

W. A. Sandby bequeathed the enormous residue of his Sandby collection to his cousin G. J. A. Peake, another great-grandson of Thomas Sandby, who in turn left them to his son, Hubert. Large portions of the collection were sold in two sales at Christie's in 1959, and in the Introduction to the catalogues of those sales attention was drawn to the fact that many items 'descended by inheritance direct from the artist, and others from the collection of Colonel W. Gravatt'.[2] Colonel Gravatt, RE, had presumably been a pupil of Paul Sandby's at Woolwich and remained on friendly terms with the artist, of whose work he formed a large collection. In W. A. Sandby's biography there are lengthy quotations from Colonel Gravatt's diary, dating from 1802, 1805 and 1807, in which Paul Sandby's methods of working in bodycolours and in oils are described.[3] Another descendant who formed a Sandby collection was Sir Charles Rich, great-grandson of both Thomas and Paul, whose widow in 1945 bequeathed a large number of drawings to Nottingham, which had already benefited considerably from the W. A. Sandby gift. Unfortunately the Rich Collection includes as many doubtful drawings as the earlier gift. It is not, perhaps, surprising that despite, or perhaps because of, W. A. Sandby's stalwart efforts on behalf of his namesakes, the reputations of Paul and Thomas Sandby fell to a low ebb during the first half of the present century, and that even Paul Oppé's pioneering work had little success in remedying the situation.

The most important representative collection of the work of Paul and Thomas Sandby created in recent years is that of Paul Mellon and the British Art Center at Yale, which will now be deservedly well-known after the impressive 1985 Exhibition, which has already been referred to. This collection has assembled some of the finest drawings that have come on to the market in the last twenty years or so, and relatively speaking the Sandby collection at Yale is on a par with their marvellous collections of Constable and Turner. It may be said that the creation of this outstanding American collection of the brothers' work reflects the fact that their relegation to a minor place in the history of British art during the first half of the present century is being made good during the second half.

NOTES

1. B. L., Cumberland Papers 36516, fol. 257.
2. Christie's, 24 March and 26 May, 1959.
3. W. A. Sandby, 1892, pp. 116–27.

Public collections with works by the Sandbys

Though not strictly speaking a 'public collection' the Royal Library at Windsor usually exhibits a selection of its prints and drawings when the Castle is open to the public, and a group of Sandby drawings is frequently included in that selection. The Sandby collection at Windsor, started by George IV when Prince of Wales, and still being added to by the Queen, is certainly the outstanding collection in existence, as regards both quality and quantity. It was brilliantly catalogued by Paul Oppé in 1947 and 1950 (see Bibliography).

The next most important assembly of prints and drawings by both Sandbys is that at the British Museum, which represents the full range of both artists' work. The majority of the drawings are listed in Vol. IV of Laurence Binyon's 1907 Catalogue, but there is no catalogue of any sort of the large number of prints, which is probably the most representative assemblage of these in the world. Nottingham, the artists' birth-place, has a large collection of their work in the Castle Museum, which is, however, of rather mixed quality. Numerous illustrations of the Nottingham drawings, and a descriptive catalogue, are included in Johnson Ball's recent *Paul and Thomas Sandby*.

There is an important selection of Paul Sandby's early Scottish drawings in the Sandby collection in the Print Room of the National Gallery of Scotland in Edinburgh, and there is another interesting selection of his work in the National Museum of Wales, in Cardiff. The Ashmolean Museum in Oxford has a representative collection, largely of Paul Sandby's works, and there is a smaller but choice group of the brothers' drawings in the Fitzwilliam Museum in Cambridge.

Largely owing to the gifts and bequests of W. A. Sandby in 1904, the work of Paul and Thomas Sandby is represented in many of the provincial art galleries and museums in Britain, though some of the individual items from his collections are of poor quality, while many others are wrongly attributed. It is this widespread distribution of doubtful drawings from an apparently reliable source that has caused such confusion in the attribution of Sandby drawings.

Many of the best Sandby drawings that have appeared on the market in the last two decades have crossed the Atlantic, and the great majority of these are now in the Paul Mellon Collection and in the collections of the Yale Center for British Art at New Haven. The range and strength of these collections, which also include large groups of prints and a few paintings, are fully demonstrated by the recent exhibition at Yale arranged and catalogued by Bruce Robertson (see Bibliography).

List of works exhibited by Paul Sandby

The following abbreviations are used:

BI: British Institution.
FSA: Free Society of Artists.
RA: Royal Academy.
SA: Society of Artists.

1760
SA

54 A view of Lord Harcourt's Seat at Newnham.
55 A Landskip, half-length.
56 Three Landskips in water-colours.

1761
SA

95 An Historical Landscape, representing the Welsh Bard in the Opening of Mr Gray's Celebrated Ode.
216 A view of Roche Abbey, at Sandbeck, Yorkshire.
217 A landscape in water-colours.
218 A small drawing of Dancing Figures.

Five Views in Scotland, viz:
219 Bonnington Linn.
220 Corhouse Linn.
221 Stonebyre Linn.
222 A view down the Clyde, from the top of Corhouse Lynn.
223 A Waterfall in the Tummel, near Killiecrankie, in the Highlands.

224 A view in North America (a print).

1762
SA

95 A view of Roche Abbey, in Yorkshire.
204 A view in the old village at Newnham in Oxfordshire.
205 A view in Blackheath.
206 An upright landscape.
207 A country operation for the Teeth.

1763
SA

111 Upper Aisgarth Foss in Wensleydale, Richmondshire, Yorks, N.R.
112 Bolton Castle, Yorks.
113 A gateway in Windsor Castle.

114 View near Whitby, in Yorks, West Riding.
115 Bothwell Castle in Clydesdale.

1764
SA

100 South-West view of Chatsworth, the seat of the Duke of Devonshire.
101 South-East view of Hackwood, seat of the Duke of Bolton.
102 View in the Menagerie at Worksop Manor, as designed by H. G. the Duchess of Norfolk.
103 The Mill near Blyth, in Yorkshire.

1765
SA

232 Entrance in to the Singing Men's Cloister, and the West End of H.M. Chapel of St George in Windsor Castle.
233 Windsor Castle from Love Lane.
234 Windsor Castle from the Gateway of a Brewhouse Yard, Datchet Lane.
235 A Moonlight.

1766
SA

146 A view on the North side of the Terrace at Windsor.

1767
SA

272 Two views of Wakefield Lodge in Whittlebury Forest, the seat of H.G. the Duke of Grafton.
273 A view of Windsor Castle from the Little Park.
272 A view of the Thames, from Mr. Munden's door at Windsor.

1768
SA

145 View of Windsor on a Rejoicing Night.
277 The Town Gate of Windsor.
278 Someries' Farm, near Luton, Beds.

SA Special Exhibition
100 View of Reading Gate; in water-colours.
101 Ditto; in ditto.

1769
RA

101 View of Roche Abbey.
102 A Bonfire.
103 The old Abbey gate, Reading.
104 The same.

1770
RA

162 View near Blackheath.
163 Charlton in Kent.
164 Another.
238-241 Morn, Noon, Evening, Night in water-colours.

1771
RA

173 A view of Bridgnorth (water-colours).
174 Bothwell Castle in Clydesdale (water-colour).
175 A Storm, from the 'Winter's Tale' (water-colours).
176 A Storm Subsiding (water-colours).

1772
RA

231 A view of Worcester (water-colours).
232 A view in Shropshire (water-colours).
233 A landscape, Sun setting (water-colours).

1773
RA

263 A view on the Thames (water-colours).
264 A view in Wales (water-colours).

1774
RA

259 The Terrace of Windsor, looking Westward.
260 The Terrace of Windsor, looking Eastward.
261 A view in Wales.
262 Bothwell Castle, in Clydesdale.
263 An upright landscape.

1775
RA

272 Manerbaur Castle in Pembrokshire (water-colour).
273 Pembroke Castle (water-colour).

274 Benton Castle, Milford Haven (water-colour).
275 Caernarvon Castle.
276 A study from nature; stained drawing.
277 A view of Windsor Castle (stained drawing).
278 do. do.
279 View of Warwick Castle; stained drawing.
280 do. do.

1776
RA

271 Part of Bangor.
272 A landscape with a recruiting party.
273 A landscape with a recruiting party – a warm evening.

1777
RA

313 The west gate of Cardiff, Glamorganshire.
314 South Gate of Cardiff, Glamorganshire.
315 A landscape in an oval.
316 Two views near Naples in aquatinta

1779
RA

284 A view of Bothwell Castle.
285 A view of Conway Castle.
286 A landscape – morning.
287 A view of Bangor; a stained drawing.

1780
RA

35 View in Wales.
89 A land storm.
192 Caernarvon Castle.
395 View in Wales.
462 Sepulchre of King Theodorick, near Ravenna (aquatinta).

1781
RA

15 View of Conway Castle.
20 View of Benton Castle.
156 View of the encampment in St. James's Park.
158 View of the encampment in the Museum Gardens.

213 View of the encampment in Hyde Park, from St. George's Row; a sketch.
367 View of the encampment in Hyde Park.
371 View of the encampment in St. James's Park.
376 View of the encampment on Blackheath.
380 View of the encampment in Hyde Park.

1782
RA
137 A Landscape.
151   do.
FSA
131 View in Millbank; a stained drawing.

1783
FSA
376 Drawing of a Landscape in bistre.

1786
RA
510 View of Woolwich.
576 St George's Gate at Canterbury.
584 The Cemetery gate at Canterbury.

1787
RA
145 Landscape; water-colours.
166   do.   do.
581   do.   do.
599 Landstorm;   do.

1788
RA
169 Landscape.
565 View in Wales.

1790
RA
495 Landscape.
623   do.

1791
RA
567 Evening view near Bayswater.
586 Morning – view on the road near Bayswater Turnpike.

1792
RA
517 Landscape.

1793
RA
541 View in the Woodyard, Windsor Great Park.
555 View at Shrewsbury.
602 View in the grove near the lodge in Windsor Great Park.
603 View in the Woodyard, Windsor Great Park.

1794
RA
328 A view of Vinters at Boxley, Kent, with Mr Whatman's Turkey Paper Mills.
367 View of Rochester Castle.
381 A view from Rochester Castle.

1795
RA
414 View of Tunbridge town and castle.
420 View of the Eagle Tower at Caernarvon.
575 Evening.
579 Morning.

1797
RA
502 View near St. Albans.
511 Landscape after a thunderstorm.

1798
RA
616 A view on the road to Hereford – a sunset.
623 A N.W. view of St. Albans – the effect of morning.
631 A view from the village of Seatoller, in Borrowdale, Cumberland.

1799
RA
650 West view of Denton Lodge, in Norfolk, the seat of Dr. Sandby, Chancellor of Norwich, Flixton House in the centre, and Flixton Hall, the seat of Mr. Alexander Adair, on the right.

658 View of Denton Lodge, in Norfolk,
the seat of Dr Sandby, etc., taken
from the road to Harleston.
662 View from Denton Lodge, Denton
Parsonage and Church, and
Aldburgh Church in the distance,
and Belvidere seat over the new
plantation.

1800
RA
367 View in Wales.
390   do.   Kent.
710 Bayswater Turnpike.
717 View near Bayswater.
734 Caernarvon Castle.

1801
RA
622 The Old Welsh Bridge at
Shrewsbury.
629 West side of the Old Welsh Bridge
at Shrewsbury.
635 East side of Bridgnorth, Shropshire.
641 Carrick Ferry, near Wexford,
Ireland.

1802
RA
600 View of Maidstone from near the
foot of Boxley Hill.
601 View on Windsor Terrace.
625 Entrance to Windsor Great Park at
Bishopsgate.

1806
RA
390 A country village.
400 A wood scene, with gypsies.
401 A study in Windsor Park.
453 Chepstow Castle.
BI
13 A wood scene, with an extensive
view in the distance.
15 A landscape composed from Nature.
78 A view of Chepstow Castle from
Percefield.

90 A view of the Old Welsh Bridge,
Shrewsbury.

1807
RA
95 Pembroke Castle looking towards
Milford Haven.
112 A beech tree.
137 Bayswater Turnpike from the east.
148 Bayswater Turnpike from the west.

1808
RA
22 A view in Windsor Forest.
27 A park scene.
54 A view of Woolwich as it was in the
year 1785.
64 A scene near Hampstead.
482 Llangollen, in Denbighshire.
565 A view of Pembroke Castle and
Town from the west.
566 Bethkellet in Caernarvonshire.
608 A forest scene.
BI
195 A landscape.
203 Chepstow Castle.
271 Part of Page's Farm, near Easton
Park, Essex.
287 Page's Farm, Easton Park, Essex,
from the west.
336 South End of Bridgnorth.
337 The Postern Gate of Canterbury.
385 Vale Crucis Abbey, near
Llangollen.
403 Bow and Arrow Castle, Portland
Island.
404 Part of Page's Farm, Essex.
422 North east view of Pembroke Castle.

1809
RA
195 A view from the back of No. 4 in
St. George's Row.
317 View of an iron forge on the River
Kent in Cumberland.
336 View of the inside of the South Gate
at Conway.
375 A view on Kilburn Road.

List of works exhibited by Thomas Sandby

1767
SA

275 Design of a country seat for a nobleman.
276 Plan of ditto.

1769
RA

99 A design in architecture.
100   do.   do.

1770
RA

161 Elevation of a country seat, for a person of distinction.

1771
RA

172 A view from the Arcade in Covent Garden.

1772
RA

230 The garden front of the Royal Academy.

1773
RA

262 A perspective view of the back part of the chapel of Windsor Great Lodge, as it appeared when built in the year 1765.

1781
RA

450 A bridge of magnificence, designed for the sixth lecture on architecture.
482 View from the entrance to the bridge, no. 450.

1782
RA

241 View of the Gothic Gallery at Strawberry Hill.

Thomas and Paul Sandby – Chronology

1717 Marriage of Thomas Sandby, framework knitter of Nottingham, to Ruth Ash.

1723 Thomas baptized in St Peter's Church, Nottingham, 8 December

1731 n.s. Paul baptized in St Peter's Church, 12 January

1742 Death of Thomas Sandby, Senior. Thomas Sandby, Junior, engaged as Military Draughtsman in the Ordnance Office in the Tower of London

1743 Thomas sent to Scotland, and present during the Duke of Cumberland's Culloden campaign, 1745-6

1746 Thomas marries Margaret Bowes

1747 n.s. In March Paul submits specimens of his work to the Board of Ordnance, and is appointed Draughtsman to the Military Survey in Scotland. Thomas now in the Netherlands, attached to the staff of the Duke of Cumberland, during the final stages of the war of the Austrian Succession

1750 Thomas appointed Draughtsman to the Duke of Cumberland, who had himself been appointed Ranger of Windsor Great Park in 1746.

c. 1752 Paul returns to London; the brothers in lodgings in Poultney Street.

1753 Thomas marries his second wife, Elizabeth Venables (*d.* 1782) – they have ten children, of whom three die young

1753-4 Paul's etchings satirizing William Hogarth published

1757 Paul marries Anne Stogden (*d.* 1797) – they have two sons and a daughter. London address now Dufours Court, Broad Street, Carnaby Market

1760 Paul shows two canvases and three watercolours at the first exhibition of the Society of Artists. *Twelve London Cries* published

1761 Thomas moves to house in Great Marlborough Street

1764 Thomas appointed Steward by Duke of Cumberland

1765 Thomas appointed Deputy Ranger of Windsor Great Park, and finally settles at Windsor. Paul shows first Windsor subjects at Society of Artists. Ryland and Byer publish collection of Paul's etchings

1766 Paul takes house in Poland Street

1768 Thomas and Paul appointed Founder Members of the Royal Academy – Paul is on the Council and Thomas is elected Professor of Architecture. Paul appointed Chief Drawing Master at the Royal Military Academy, Woolwich, and when there lives in lodgings at Old Charlton, Kent

1769 Thomas competes for the Royal exchange at Dublin, winning the third premium. Paul on Hanging Committee of first RA Exhibition, himself showing four works

1770 Paul's first recorded visit to Wales, as guest of Sir Watkin Williams-Wynn – in 1771 tours North Wales with Sir Watkin

1772 Paul moves to 4 St George's Row, Bayswater, his home for the rest of his life

1773 Paul tours in Wales with Joseph Banks and the Hon. Charles Greville

1775 Paul engraves and publishes his first aquatints, *XII Views in South Wales*. Thomas commissioned to design the Freemasons' Hall in Queen Street, Lincoln's Inn Fields, and is appointed Grand Architect of the Order of Freemasons

1776 Paul publishes three further sets of aquatints: *Views of Warwick Castle*, *Views of Windsor* and *XII Views in North Wales*

1777 Thomas appointed Architect of the King's Works

1778 *The Virtuosi's Museum* published; reissued in 1781 by John Boydell as *One Hundred and Fifty Select Views in England, Scotland and Ireland*

1780 Paul makes numerous drawings of the military encampments in and around London after the Gordon Riots, and bases several series of aquatints and engravings on them. Thomas appointed Master Carpenter in the Office of Works, a post abolished in 1782

1781 Thomas exhibits two designs for his *Bridge of Magnificence* at the RA

1786 Thomas Paul Sandby, Paul's second son, marries Harriot, Thomas's second surviving daughter – they live with Thomas at Windsor, and have a large family

1793 Paul decorates the dining room at Drakelow Hall, Derbyshire, for Sir Nigel Gresley, Bart. Lt Paul Sandby, Paul's eldest son, dies at Barbados

1796 Paul resigns his post at Woolwich, and is succeeded by his second son, Thomas Paul

1797 6 November, death of Paul's wife, Anne

1798 25 June, death of Thomas, after some years of illness; buried at Windsor. Thomas Paul and his family move to Englefield Green, near Egham, Surrey

1799 Sale of Thomas's drawings and books by Leigh and Sotheby's, starting 18 July. Paul appointed acting Librarian at RA

1809 7 November, death of Paul; buried at St George's, Hanover Square

1811 Sale of Paul's paintings and drawings, Christie's, 2–4 May; the first of several sales arranged by Thomas Paul

Catalogue of watercolours and drawings by Paul Sandby in the collection of the Victoria & Albert Museum

The drawings are arranged in a chronological order; for those that are not dated an approximate date is proposed. Sizes are given in inches and centimetres, height before width.

Catalogue

1

'Prospect of the Entrance into the Tower taken from the back of the Stone Kitchen'

Pen and ink and grey wash, on white laid paper; $11\frac{3}{8} \times 16\frac{1}{4}$ ($28\cdot5 \times 41\cdot2$)
Drawing surrounded by thin and thick black line borders. Inscribed below, at left, in ink, *Paul Sandby delin. 1746.7*, and with title along lower margin of sheet; to left of this, in pencil, *20*, and to right, in ink, in a copperplate hand, *presented to the Board as a/ Specimen of his performance/vide Minutes 12 Mar*, and completed in pencil, *1746*. On *verso*, in black chalk, *Sandby 1746/Colonel Scotts(wall)*.

E1119–1931

CONDITION: Join at centre, and several tears, especially at margins; somewhat rubbed and spotted, but overall in reasonable condition.
PROV: Purchased 1931 (Bernard Squire, £6.6.0)
EXH: Australia, City of Hamilton and elsewhere, *Paul Sandby Drawings*, October 1981–March 1982, No. 1.
LIT: M. Hardie, *Water-colour Painting in Britain*, Vol. 1, 1966, p. 99.

In the left foreground are the Entrance buildings, reflected in the water of the moat below them; to right, various houses and another gateway with two sentinel boxes.

When compared with the set of eight related drawings in the British Museum (L. B. 102–7), it seems clear that while these, with the exception of the frontispiece (L. B. 102a), are delicate pen and ink drawings carefully copied from prints and prepared as a 'portfolio' for submission to the Board of Ordnance in support of Paul Sandby's application for employment, **1** is totally different in character and technique. It seems probable that it was an 'on-the-spot' drawing executed at the request of the Board as a demonstration of the young artist's topographical skills. The BM drawings bear the same copper-plate inscription as **1**, recording their presentation to the Board. Paul Sandby's application was successful, and he became the official draughtsman to the Military Survey in Scotland in 1747. At this time the Board of Ordnance Drawing Room was located in the Tower of London; the Stone Kitchen was one of the public houses located near the Tower.

2
The removal from the Thames at The Bells of Ouseley of the hulk which became the Chinese Junk on Virginia Water

Bodycolour; $13 \times 24\frac{3}{4}$ (33×63) – sight.
113–1898
(see also colour plate between pp. 64 and 65)
CONDITION: Considerable flaking in numerous places, especially on both sides of an old fold in the centre
PROV: Purchased in 1898 (£25)
EXH: Guildhall Art Gallery, *Paul Sandby Exhibition*, 1960, No. 1; Reading and Bolton, *Paintings and Drawings by Thomas and Paul Sandby*, 1972, No. 31.
LIT: T. E. Harwood, *Windsor, Old and New*, 1929, repr. facing p. 256; P. Oppé, *Sandby Drawings at Windsor Castle*, 1947, p. 41.

At right of centre the hulk is being drawn up the river bank by numerous teams of oxen, driven by men on foot and on horseback. In the foreground there is a dense crowd of men, women, children and various animals; to left, a single tree and wooden steps leading up from it to the inn. Below the tree, to right, a green-coated figure said to represent the Duke of Cumberland is directing the operation, and close to him is an enormously fat woman with a vast hooped skirt. In the middle distance and distance are more figures, houses and trees.

The event depicted took place around 1752, as the Chinese Junk appears complete in an engraving dated 1753 and in the Sandbys' *Eight Views of Windsor* of 1754. There are several related drawings in the Royal Collection (Oppé, Nos. 117 and 118 – repr. pl. 56 – and Nos. 407–9); of these No. 118 is clearly a preliminary study used in the execution of the present work. Like this preliminary study, which is inscribed on the *verso* in Paul Sandby's hand, **2** can be confidently attributed to Paul, though in the past the possible involvement of Thomas has also been mooted. It is difficult to propose a firm date, but *c.* 1755 would seem feasible. This date is confirmed by the similarity in execution of the large tree on the left with that in the centre of the bodycolour drawing of *Woodcutters near a River*, which is signed and dated *1756*, in the Corporation of London's Collection (see Guildhall Art Gallery, *Paul Sandby*, 1960, No. 12, repr.).

3
Landscape with mill-house, tower and stream

Watercolour varnished; $2\frac{3}{4} \times 7\frac{7}{8}$ (7×20)
123-1894
CONDITION: Good
PROV: Given by Mr J. E. Taylor, 1894

The stream is in the centre, with the mill-house on the right bank and the round tower beside a gateway on the left. A woman is driving cattle through the gate.

A delicate drawing with fine nuances of colour in the sky. The attribution seems plausible and a date around 1760 is likely.

The scene appears to be a Continental one.

4
The Old Bridge at Windsor

Watercolour and pen and ink, on white
laid paper, with considerable uncoloured
areas, stuck down on a thin board with
grey line-wash borders; $10\frac{1}{8} \times 16\frac{5}{8}$ ($25·8 \times$
$42·2$); the old mount, $12\frac{1}{8} \times 18\frac{1}{2}$ ($30·7 \times 47$)
201–1894 (see also colour plate between
pp. 64 and 65)
CONDITION: Good (after recent restoration)
with some repairs at margins and in sky
PROV: Purchased in 1894
LIT: Repr. *The Studio*, LXXII (1918),
p. 141, illustrating an article by Frank
Gibson on 'Paul and Thomas Sandby';
there attributed to Thomas Sandby

The timber bridge, on a series of timber
supports, extends across the river in the
centre of the composition, with houses at
each end; on it are a coach and horses and
numerous other figures, some mounted; in
the water, in left foreground, a four-oared
boat flying an ensign and with passengers
below a canopy in the stern; a punt at the
river bank on right, and on this, in the
foreground, a group of two men, a woman
and two girls (one of whom is fishing)
beneath a tall brick wall.

In the past this drawing has been
attributed to either Paul or Thomas, but
there seems no reason to doubt that it is
the work of Paul, dating from *c.* 1760. A
version of the same composition, with only
slight variations in detail, is in the Eton
College Collection.

5
Classical landscape

Bodycolour; $7\frac{1}{8} \times 10\frac{3}{4}$ (18×27.4) – sight
1729–1900
CONDITION: Good, except for some scuffing
marks at upper margin in the sky
PROV: Bequeathed by H. S. Ashbee in 1900

In the left foreground there is a
meandering stream, with a woman and
child by its bank in centre foreground; to
right, a group of spindly trees and, in
centre middle distance, a village
surrounding a castle. In the distance a
range of mountains is shown, with a peak
to right of centre. The sky is largely clear,
with sparse clouds.

An Italianate scene in the tradition of
Marco Ricci, some gouaches by whom
were owned by Paul Sandby. **No. 5** is in
keeping with the earlier gouache drawings
of Paul Sandby, executed in the 1760s.

6

The three daughters of the 2nd Earl of Waldegrave with Miss Keppel and a governess

Watercolour over touches of pencil, on thin white tracing paper, stuck down on white laid paper; $5\frac{1}{8} \times 7\frac{1}{8}$ ($13 \times 18\cdot1$) – the supporting paper, $6 \times 7\frac{5}{8}$ ($15\cdot2 \times 19\cdot3$) Inscribed, in pencil, below each figure (other than the governess) from left to right *1 2 3 4*; and below the drawing on the supporting paper *1 Miss Keppel Daughter of the Bishop of Exeter/2 Lady Laura Walgrave/3 Lady Horatia Walgrave/4 Lady Maria Walgrave* (*de* is added above the name *Walgrave* in each case). There are additional later inscriptions on the *verso* of the mount and on an old label preserved with the drawing, but these vary from the inscription cited, which may be by Paul Sandby himself.
D 1835–1904
(see also colour plate between pp. 64 and 65)
CONDITION: Good, with some slight rubbing at edges and corners
PROV: Bequeathed by W. A. Sandby in 1904
EXH: Nottingham Castle, 1884, No. 135; Phoenix, Utah, San Diego, Toronto, Ottawa and Victoria, *Forty-two British Watercolours from the V & A*, 1977, No. 4; Australia, City of Hamilton and elsewhere; *Paul Sandby Drawings*; October 1981–March 1982; No. 78.
LIT: C. Monkhouse, *Earlier English Watercolour Painters*, 1890, repr. p. 3; V. Bidulph, *The Three Ladies Waldegrave*, 1938, repr.; Paul Oppé, *The Drawings of Paul and Thomas Sandby in the Collection of His Majesty the King at Windsor Castle*, 1947, pp. 49 and 71; M. Hardie, *Water-colour Painting in Britain*, Vol. 1, 1966, p. 109

The governess is standing between the two youngest girls in the centre of the composition, with the two elder girls at the left; behind them are indications of a wall, the corner of a building and a distant landscape.

There has been some difficulty about the identification of the figures in this drawing, which must rest on the old inscription cited above. The daughters of the 2nd Earl of Waldegrave (who had married as his second wife, on 15 May 1759, Maria Walpole, the illegitimate daughter of Sir Edward Walpole by Dorothy Clementi, a milliner's apprentice) were: Elizabeth Laura, *b.* 1760, who married her cousin George, 4th Earl of Waldegrave, 5 May 1782 – she is no. 2 in the drawing; Charlotte Maria, *b.* 1761, who married George Henry Earl of Euston and 4th Duke of Grafton, 16 Nov. 1784 – she is numbered 4; Anna Horatia, b. 1762, who ultimately married Lord Hugh Seymour and is numbered 3 in the drawing. The Miss Keppel was the eldest daughter of the Bishop, the Hon. Frederick Keppel, and she was Anna Maria (*b.* 1759) and a cousin of the Waldegrave girls. Her mother Laura was the elder sister of Maria, the Countess Waldegrave. Both these ladies have been suggested for identification with the adult figure in the drawing, but the plainness of that figure's dress would seem to indicate that she was a governess. The three Waldegrave girls, who were grand-nieces of Horace Walpole, were portrayed by Sir Joshua Reynolds in 1781 (E. K. Waterhouse, *Reynolds*, 1961, p. 72 and pl. 222; the portrait is now in the National Gallery of Scotland). The age of the girls would indicate a date of *c.* 1770 for **6**, though on stylistic grounds an earlier date has been suggested.

A related study is at Windsor (Oppé no. 296, pl. 119). This omits the governess and the youngest girl, but includes the space they would have occupied, and has slight variations in detail in the three girls portrayed; the background landscape is omitted. Oppé's identification of the figures in the Windsor and V & A drawings is faulty, but he points out that they recur in several finished compositions. The two elder girls are included in a group in an aquatint of 1776, *The North Terrace looking Westward*; the governess and Lady Maria are seen accompanied by a gentleman in the left foreground of Thomas Sandby's

Old Somerset House, the Garden or river front in the Royal Collection (Oppé, no. 163); and the whole group is repeated in a large gouache of *The North Terrace looking East,* formerly in the collection of Mrs Angerstein. Thus though **5** may have begun as portraiture, it was clearly used by Paul Sandby as one of his reference stock of figure studies always at hand when he required staffage figures for his compositions. Furthermore, the faces of the four girls are almost identical in their features, and the quality of this study lies rather in its harmonious grouping and colouring than in its success in portraying individual characteristics.

7
Two horses

Watercolour over pencil, on white laid paper; $4\frac{3}{4} \times 7\frac{1}{2}$ ($12 \cdot 2 \times 19$)
Inscribed in pencil with one or two colour notes near the horse on right
P 2–1977
CONDITION: Somewhat faded around the larger horse, which has been, and still is, the only one seen when the mount is closed
PROV: Bequeathed by Mrs N. E. F. Beattie in 1977

A sleek chestnut hunter, its head slightly inclined, is shown in left foreground; in the right middle distance, a black nag with a short tail and a saddle on its back.
A fluent study of *c.* 1770.

8
Two putti using compasses

Pencil and some wash on white paper; $2\frac{1}{2} \times 4\frac{1}{8}$ ($6 \cdot 5 \times 10 \cdot 5$)
Inscribed at lower left, in pencil, *F.*
E 776–1963
CONDITION: Somewhat marked and rubbed
PROV: Col. Gravatt; William Sandby; Hubert Peake (Christie's, 26.5.1959); Mrs K. J. E. Bostrom, by whom presented in 1963

In the centre is a stone slab or table with a celestial globe standing on it; the putto at left is standing and leaning over the table, the compass in his right hand; the putto at right is seated on the table, his left leg resting on the ground, the compass in his right hand. In the distance, at centre, a slight sketch of a ship.
This is presumably a study for an emblematic drawing or print, which dates from about 1770; there is a related study in the Carr Album. So far there has been no satisfactory explanation of the significance of the 'F' inscribed on this drawing, and numerous other figure drawings by Paul Sandby, including a considerable number in the Carr Album, catalogued under **52** below. There is a discussion of this mark on page 20 of Paul Oppé's work on the Sandby drawings at Windsor Castle.

9
Eton College and Windsor from the Playing Fields

Watercolour with some bodycolour, over pencil, on white laid paper, stuck down on a green and pink line wash mount; $14\frac{1}{8} \times 27\frac{3}{4}$ (36×70.5)
An elegant copperplate inscription removed from the old mount in 1977 reads *View of the Castle Town and College from the Play-fields.*
D 1833-1904
(see also colour plate – between pp. 64 and 65)
CONDITION: Good – cleaned and restored in 1977
PROV: Sir Joseph Banks (according to ink inscription on *verso* recorded in 1904 Register); bequeathed by W. A. Sandby in 1904
EXH: Nottingham Castle, 1884, No. 212; Guildhall Art Gallery, *Paul Sandby*, 1960, No. 43
LIT: A. W. Rich, *Water Colour Painting*, 1918, pl. XLIV

The red brick College buildings are to the right, the castle and town across the river to the left. In left foreground, cattle are browsing below a birch tree; to right, a group of trees with a gentleman reading, leaning against the trunk of one of them, and another gentleman resting on the ground at his feet. A luminous sky with some clouds.

An outstanding drawing of *c.* 1770, comparable in its harmonious tonality and colouring with the best examples from the Banks Collection at Windsor. According to the 1884 Nottingham Exhibition catalogue, the two figures on the right are alleged to depict the artist reading and his brother Thomas reclining on the grass.

10
Windsor Castle: the North Terrace looking west, at sunset

Bodycolour on primed mahogany panel;
$18\frac{1}{4} \times 24\frac{1}{4}$ ($46 \cdot 4 \times 61 \cdot 5$)
P 7–1945
CONDITION: Good
PROV: Mrs Norman (in 1843); Miss
Georgiana Angerstein (Holbrook House,
Wincanton, Somerset; one of a set of three
times of day – the others *Morning* and
Afternoon); purchased 1945 (Leggatt's,
£320)
EXH: Guildhall Art Gallery, *Paul Sandby*,
1960, No. 41

The North Terrace, showing the west end
of Queen Elizabeth's Gallery, Winchester
Tower and the Canons' Houses, with
numerous figures, in groups and single, at
various points on the terrace; most notably
a group of two women, four children and a
dog in right foreground. A cloudy sky with
the setting sun partially seen above a layer
of cloud in the centre of the composition.

A striking and beautifully executed
example of this favourite Windsor Castle
composition, of which there are numerous
other versions, including **14** and **34** below.
It dates from about 1770.

11
Caesar's Tower and part of Warwick Castle from the Island

Watercolour over pencil, on white laid paper; 20 × 30 (50·8 × 76·2)
Signed and dated, in ink, on rock at lower right, *P. Sandby 1775*
814–1877
(see also colour plate between pp. 64 and 65)
CONDITION: Somewhat faded overall, with a few slight tears at margins
PROV: Purchased in 1877 (Hogarth & Sons, £21)
EXH: ?RA 1775, No. 279 or 280; Reading and Bolton, *Paintings and Drawings by Thomas and Paul Sandby*, 1972, No. 48

At left the stark façade of the Castle, with Caesar's Tower to the right, rises above the River Avon; from it a low stone building with a water-wheel juts out into the river, where the weir crosses it. To right, further back, is the bridge, with houses and trees

beyond. In centre foreground, a man at the water's edge is axing a fallen tree being held down by a woman and a boy; a dog is shown to the right.

Paul Sandby exhibited two drawings of Warwick Castle at the Royal Academy in 1775 (Nos. 279 and 280); the present impressive drawing is very probably one of these. This composition was the basis of plate 3 of Paul Sandby's *Four Views of Warwick Castle*, a set of sepia aquatints published by Boydell in 1775–6. There are only minor variations between the drawing and the aquatint, which is, however, considerably smaller, measuring $12\frac{3}{4} \times 18\frac{5}{8}$ (32·5 × 47·2) The present composition is not the one engraved by J. Fittler in 1780 as plate LXXI of *The Virtuosi's Museum*, as suggested in the V & A Print Room Catalogue. Sandby made numerous drawings of Warwick Castle, and among other versions of this composition is one dated 1801 in the City of Hamilton Art Gallery, Australia.

12
Chepstow Castle

Watercolour over pencil, on thin laid board; $11\frac{1}{2} \times 20\frac{7}{8}$ (29·2 × 53)
Signed and dated at lower left, in ink, *P. Sandby 1775*. Inscribed in pencil, at centre of *verso*; *This drawing was done for Chase Price/I purchased it at the Bernard sale at/ (Gravesend) 21 Feb 87 – Paul Sandby retouched it for/me Nov 88 – & said in His humourous Manner/'He in red by the Boat Mr Greville. He in blue going/down to (harbour) is me up to my knees in mud'/ . . . Nov 88*. [The writing is difficult to decipher; words in brackets are uncertain, and the monogram signature is indecipherable.] Below this inscription, in a different hand, also in pencil *Given to Mr Copeland by Lady Ford 1829*; and at top right, in ink *(BB)* [illegible monogram] *No. 1044/ 21 by 11$\frac{1}{2}$*
613–1870
CONDITION: Somewhat faded and rubbed at several places, especially in the sky
PROV: Price; Lady Ford; Copeland (see inscriptions above); bequeathed by J. M. Parsons in 1870

The largely ruinous buildings of the castle are at the centre and to the right, at the top of the rocky bank of the River Wye. To the left is the wooden bridge across the river, with the far bank beyond. In the centre foreground a rowing boat is drawn up on the bank with four figures in and near it: two rowing boats at centre of river. Engraved in aquatint by Paul Sandby as the first plate in *XII Views . . . in South Wales*, published in 1775. The plate (see Fig. 14) is dated *Sepr. 1st 1775*, and gives a slightly reduced version of the drawing, omitting also a small section at left. The foreground staffage figures are identical, but in place of the two sailing boats the print has one six-oared rowing boat. If it were not for the inscription on the *verso* the boats and figures, which are very feebly drawn, would be difficult to attribute to Paul Sandby himself. However, the inscriptions appear authentic and provide evidence that on occasions the artist could include very inferior staffage figures in his compositions.

13
Hubberstone Priory, near Milford Haven

Watercolour and pen and ink, on white paper, stuck down on thin board, with a grey line-washed border; $5\frac{1}{8} \times 7\frac{1}{4}$ (13×18.5); the mount $7\frac{7}{8} \times 9\frac{1}{4}$ (18.2×23.5)
Inscribed lightly in pencil below drawing on the mount, *Hubberston Priory near Milford Haven*, and at lower left of mount, *P. Sandby* (perhaps a signature). On *verso* of the old mount, in ink, *by Sandby 1780*, and other inscriptions which give the title, etc.
Dyce 747
CONDITION: Good
PROV: William Dyce Bequest, 1869

In the foreground are two arms of a stream with an island in the middle and a low weir on the right. The buildings of the priory, partly ruinous, are on far bank to right; a wooded hill in the background, and in left foreground a man and a woman conversing, also a dog and a cow with calf.

A harmonious drawing of *c.* 1775, with fine effects of light and shade. The engraving by T. Mazel, dated *Dec. 1, 1778*, is Plate 33 of *The Virtuosi's Museum*, and exactly reproduces the drawing (see Fig. 16). The Benedictine Priory of Pill (in the Parish of Hubberstone, now Milford) was founded *c.* 1170 by Adam de Rupe, and was subordinate to the Abbey of St Dogmael in north Pembrokeshire.

14
Windsor Terrace looking westward

Outline etching with grey and some coloured washes; $11\frac{1}{2} \times 17\frac{5}{8}$ (29·2 × 44·8) Inscribed in pencil at lower right corner *321*; and on *verso*, in ink, *Terrace Windsor Castle P Sandby Esq.*, and, in pencil, various geometric doodles
Dyce 745
CONDITION: Some slight tears at margins; an old fold across centre from left to right; several scratches and some rubbing
PROV: William Dyce Bequest, 1869

The North Terrace, showing the west end of Queen Elizabeth's Gallery, Winchester Tower, and the Canons' Houses at left, with numerous figures walking and conversing on the terrace in the foreground. On the right, a broad view of the Thames Valley below.

This washed etching could well be Sandby's own preliminary attempt at working out the lights and shadows before proceeding to apply aquatint to his plate. The completed aquatint was published on 1 September 1776, and the lights and shadows in the present sheet closely resemble those in the completed print. For other versions of this view in the Museum see **10** and **34**; numerous further versions are to be found in the Royal Collection and elsewhere.

15
Llandaff Cathedral

Watercolour with pen and ink over traces of pencil, with some heightening with white, on white laid paper; $12 \times 18\frac{1}{8}$ ($30 \cdot 5 \times 46$)
FA 554
CONDITION: Considerably faded
PROV: Bought before 1860
EXH: Society of Arts, *Historical Water-Colour Paintings*, 1861

The Cathedral, seen from the south-east, occupies the left and centre of the composition; a single tree on right, with road and houses among trees beyond.

A precise and rather toneless drawing (in which a ruler may have been used), probably dating from *c.* 1775. The same composition, on a reduced scale and with some variations in staffage, etc., was engraved by W. Watts as Plate 23 of *The Virtuosi's Museum*; the plate is dated 1 September 1778. The composition is also repeated in an aquatint plate of Llandaff, engraved and published by Paul Sandby in September 1777 (altered to 1779 in the B.M. impression, 1904 – 8 – 19 – 690).

16
Village street, Old Charlton, Kent

Watercolour and pen and ink, on laid
paper, stuck down on board; $12\frac{1}{8} \times 20\frac{1}{4}$
(30.7×51.5)
815–1877
CONDITION: Considerably faded and
darkened overall; surface rubbed at several
places in the sky
PROV: Purchased in 1877 (Hogarth & Sons,
£8. 8. 0)

A group of houses and cottages is shown on
the left, the first with four large and
complex brick chimneys. There are several
figures on the pavement in front of the
houses, including a red-coated man seated
with his back against a paling fence at left.
The street is in the centre, lined by trees in
the distance: to the right, a large tree, and
a house behind a paling fence.

A fine drawing in poor condition, which
dates from the later 1770s. A less finished
version of this composition, with only slight
variations and of the same size, was sold at
Christie's on 26 May 1959 (lot 20); this
was formerly in the collections of William
Sandby and Herbert Peake. Paul Sandby
had lodgings at Charlton while he was
employed at the Royal Military Academy
at Woolwich from 1768 to 1796.

17
Old Tea Gardens near the Bridge,
Bayswater Road

Watercolour with pen and ink, on laid
paper; $7\frac{3}{8} \times 10\frac{3}{8}$ ($18\cdot7 \times 26\cdot3$); stuck down on
old mount with grey line wash borders
Inscribed at bottom of old mount, in
pencil, *In the Garden of the Tavern at
Bayswater*; and on the *verso* of the mount,
also in pencil, *View near the Bridge over
Bayswater, looking to the Entrance from the
West.* In ink, in another hand, *by Paul
Sandby R.A.*, and *£2. 2. 0 each/or 3. 3. 0 the
pair* and various stock numbers, etc., in
pencil
12–1887
CONDITION: Somewhat faded and dirty
overall
PROV: Purchased in 1887 (£6. 6. 0)
EXH: Guildhall Art Gallery, *Paul Sandby*,
1960, No.56.

At the left there are various buildings and
a path between wooden palings, among
trees; on the right, three men seated at a
table beneath a tree, with more trees and a
pond beyond them.

This drawing forms a pair with **18**; see
the note to this. No. P 16–1952 in the
collection is a weak nineteenth-century
copy of this composition, slightly reduced
and in pencil and watercolour. There is a
drawing of the *Flora Tea Gardens* at the
British Museum (L. B. 22), which is similar
in manner though showing a different
view.

18

Old Public House, Bayswater

Watercolour with pen and ink, on laid paper; $7\frac{1}{4} \times 10\frac{1}{4}$ (18·5 × 26); stuck down on old mount with grey line-wash borders
Inscribed on *verso* of the old mount, in pencil, *Back of the Public House near Bayswater;* in ink, in another hand, *by Paul Sandby R.A.*, and £2.2.0 each/£3.3.0 the *Pair*
13–1887
CONDITION: Somewhat faded and dirty overall
PROV: Purchased in 1887 (£6.6.0)
EXH: Guildhall Art Gallery, *Paul Sandby*, 1960, No. 60; Australia, City of Hamilton and elsewhere; *Paul Sandby Drawings*; October 1981–March 1982; No. 31.

The front of the inn is on the right; in centre foreground, a woman with two children and a dog; to the left, three men drinking, seated beneath a large tree near a fence. In the centre distance, a large house is seen among trees beyond a brick wall.

This pair of Bayswater views is drawn and coloured with some freedom, and dates from about 1780. Paul Sandby acquired 4 St George's Row, just off Bayswater Road in Paddington, in 1772, and lived there until the end of his life.

19

Landscape with mountains by a lake

Watercolour over pencil on laid paper;
$10\frac{1}{4} \times 14\frac{1}{2}$ (26 × 36·8)
P 6-1959
CONDITION: Good
PROV: Col. Gravatt (Oct. 1867); William
Sandby; Hubert Peake (Christie's,
26.5.1959, lot 79); purchased through
Thos. Agnew & Sons, 1959.

EXH: International Exhibitions Foundation,
*British Watercolors from the Victoria and Albert
Museum*, 1966–7, No. 81

A range of mountains beyond a lake with
one or two groups of buildings on its far
bank. In the foreground a track among
rocks and trees, with a man seated on a
rock to left of centre.

A fluent composition of the 1780s.

20
Dolbadern Castle

Watercolour and pen and ink, on white rag paper; $10\frac{3}{4} \times 16\frac{1}{4}$ ($27\cdot3 \times 41\cdot3$), sight
P 28-1963
CONDITION: Slightly faded and rubbed
PROV: Thos. Agnew & Sons (label on back of frame); Mrs L. H. Beattie, by whom presented in 1963.

The round tower of the castle is in the centre of the composition, with the lake in the foreground and mountains behind. In the left foreground there is a slender tree, with two men seated below it, fishing.

This is something of a 'stock' drawing of the 1780s. The aquatint view of Llanberis Lake and Dolbadern Castle published as plate 10 in *Views in North Wales* in 1776 is taken from a more distant point.

21
The Round Temple

Watercolour over pencil, on white laid
paper, stuck down on paper with a pink,
grey and yellow wash surround; $10\frac{3}{8} \times 14\frac{3}{8}$
$(26\cdot4 \times 36\cdot5)$; original mount $14\frac{1}{2} \times 18$
$(36\cdot8 \times 45\cdot7)$
Signed and dated in pen and ink on rock
in centre foreground, P *Sandby 1788*.
Inscribed in pencil at bottom left of the old
mount, *Round Temple P. Sandby*, and on
back of the old mount, *Paul Sandby*, both in
nineteenth-century hands.
FA 561
(see also colour plate between pp. 64 and
65)
CONDITION: Good, though slightly faded
PROV: Purchased before 1860
EXH: International Exhibitions Foundation,
*British Watercolors from the Victoria and Albert
Museum*, 1966–7, No. 80

The temple, with two figures genuflecting
before it, is among trees on the left;
beyond, to the right, a bay with mountains
on the skyline and classical buildings on
islands; to the right, trees and a steep cliff.

A pleasantly balanced Claude-like
composition, with fine tonal values.

22

A road in mountainous country, leading to a castle by a lake

Watercolour with pen and ink on laid paper; $9\frac{5}{8} \times 14\frac{1}{4}$ (24·5 × 36·2)
P 5-1959
CONDITION: Good, except for one or two damages in the sky at right of centre
PROV: Col. Gravatt (Sept. 1867); William Sandby; Hubert Peake (Christie's, 26.5.1959, lot 87); purchased through Thos. Agnew & Sons, 1959.

In left foreground is a group of trees with the lake below and beyond them; to right the road with a horseman, a man on foot and a dog at the brow of the hill. Beyond, mountains on right, with the castle below them on the lakeside at centre.

A crisp and fluent composition, certainly imaginary, of the late 1780s.

23
Rye House, Hoddesdon, Hertfordshire
Watercolour over pencil on white laid
paper, $8\frac{1}{2} \times 13\frac{1}{2}$ ($21\cdot6 \times 34\cdot3$)
E 810-1939
CONDITION: Considerably faded and damp-
stained in sky
PROV: Presented by Messrs Frank Partridge
& Sons, Ltd, in 1939

The gatehouse is in the centre, topped by a
smoking chimney, with a view over open
wooded country to the left, and a lake in
the middle distance. In the foreground, a
stunted tree on left, and a group of trees on
right; to left of centre a two-wheeled cart
drawn by two horses with the carter beside
them.

A run-of-the-mill drawing of the later
1780s. The gatehouse is all that remains of
Rye House, which was the venue of the
Rye House Plot against Charles II in 1683.

24
'Morning: View on the Road near Bayswater Turnpike' (The 'Old Swan', Bayswater)

Watercolour over pencil, on laid paper;
$25\frac{1}{2} \times 35$ (64·8 × 89)
Signed and dated, in ink, on the back of a cart in right foreground, *P. Sandby 1790*, and inscribed on signpost at right, *Bayswater*
D 1831–1904
(see also colour plate between pp. 64 and 65)
CONDITION: Generally faded and dirty; numerous rust (?foxing) spots
PROV: Presented by W. A. Sandby in 1904
EXH: RA, 1791, No. 586; Nottingham Castle, 1884, No. 157; Guildhall Art Gallery, *Paul Sandby*, 1960, No. 42

The white turnpike gates are in the centre, with two mounted gentlemen and two ladies on foot approaching. The inn is at left, with numerous figures in front of it, including three men mixing mortar, a servant girl carrying out food and drink, and a group of soldiers drinking beneath a slender tree in the centre. On the other side of the road are numerous and varied trees behind a park wall, besides which, at extreme right, a group of five laundresses with laden baskets on their heads are walking towards the turnpike. In the right foreground is a two-wheeled cart laden with barrels, and with two men seated in it, one having his clay-pipe lit by a girl holding a candle.

This impressive *tour de force* is certainly the Bayswater subject exhibited at the RA in 1791 as No. 586; No. 567 in the same exhibition was *Evening: View near Bayswater*. There is a study of the cart and figures on and near it in the right foreground at the British Museum (L. B. 138, No. 14). Another drawing in the same album (L. B. 138, No. 22) includes a study of men mixing mortar related to the group in the left foreground. A study of the group of washerwomen is at Yale (B 1977.14.5133).

25
An ancient beech tree

Bodycolour on paper; $26\frac{1}{2} \times 40$ ($67\cdot3 \times 101\cdot6$), sight
Signed and dated in ink, on a root at the base of the tree, *P. Sandby 1794*
FA 383
(see also colour plate between pp. 64 and 65)
CONDITION: Good
PROV: Purchased before 1860
EXH: ?RA, 1795, No. 579; Tokyo, National Museum of Western Art, *European Landscape Painting*, 1978, No. 42.
LIT: Richard and Samuel Redgrave, *A Century of British Painters*, new edition 1947, p. 151; C. Hussey, *The Picturesque*, 1927, repr. facing p. 128

The gnarled trunk of the tree is at right of centre, and it opens out into numerous quite sparsely leaved branches, to dominate the upper half of the composition. Behind, at right, is a dense wood, and to left a river or lake with wooded banks and mountains beyond. There are some boats on the water and various buildings on the shores. Below the tree, to right, are two men, one of them holding a hat full of ?mushrooms, and a girl; to left a seated dog is guarding a hat on the ground, and beyond the dog is a group of three horses. Below the tree at left there is a track, on which is a donkey cart with a man and a woman in it.

This powerful composition is one of the most striking of Paul Sandby's large-scale gouache works of the later years of his career. A similar composition with much more detailed buildings in the distance is at the British Art Center at Yale (B 1983.9.1). This has been identified as a view of Bridgnorth on the River Severn in Shropshire, and dated about 1801.

26
A view of the Keeper's Lodge, Easton Park, Suffolk

Bodycolour on ?blue paper, stuck down on thin board with a single grey line border; $8 \times 10\frac{7}{8}$ ($20 \cdot 3 \times 27 \cdot 6$); the mount $9 \times 12\frac{3}{8}$ ($22 \cdot 8 \times 31 \cdot 5$)
Inscribed in pencil on the *verso* of the old mount *N W View of the Keeper's Lodge/Easton Park/by P Sandby R A Deceased*
Dyce 746
CONDITION: Somewhat rubbed and spotted all over
PROV: William Dyce Bequest, 1869

The lodge and its outbuildings are at left, with trees behind and a wood to the right; in the foreground, a meadow with cattle grazing.

A work of the 1790s, of better quality in the trees than in the buildings and animals. Another, but different, view of the Keeper's Lodge is in the British Museum (L. B. 38). In the eighteenth century Easton Park, which is near Wickham Market, was a seat of the Wingfield and Nassau families.

27
Scene in Windsor Forest
Watercolour over pencil, on thin rag
board; $9\frac{3}{8} \times 11\frac{5}{8}$ ($23\cdot8 \times 29\cdot5$)
P 7–1959
CONDITION: Slightly faded; rubbed in one or
two places at right
PROV: Col. Gravatt (Aug., 1867); William
Sandby; Hubert Peake (Christie's,
26.5.1959, part of lot 39); purchased
through Thos. Agnew & Sons, 1959.

A forest clearing with fallen trees in the
foreground – a timber cart loaded with a
hefty tree trunk is shown at right.

This sheet belongs to the large number
of Windsor Woodyard and similar scenes
that Paul Sandby drew in the 1790s.

28
Dragoons galloping along the road at Vanbrugh Fields, Greenwich

Bodycolour on board, with single black line border; $12\frac{1}{4} \times 10\frac{3}{8}$ (31·1 × 26·3)
Signed (almost erased) at lower left, *P Sandby (RA)*. Inscribed, in pen and ink, in a contemporary hand, on an old label attached to the current mount, *Dragoons – painted by Paul Sandby RA in bodycolour 1794/ heightened with Crayon and should be kept glazed. for Ann Cobbe.*
416–1885
CONDITION: Good (after recent restoration), but with the remains of some scratches and stains in the sky
PROV: Ann Cobbe; purchased in 1885 (J.J.R. Green, £7)
EXH: National Gallery, Washington, and Metropolitan Museum, New York, *English Drawings and Water Colors from British Collections*, No. 71

In the right foreground four dragoons, all mounted on brown horses, are galloping up a broad roadway towards the gatehouse in the middle distance; to the left are a woman with a child and a dog, a man with a laden donkey, a horse and covered cart, and beyond this two further dragoons. At left there is a tall brick wall with trees behind, and at right a park with Vanbrugh's House between trees. A pink and yellow tinted sunset sky.

A fair example of the rather freer gouache compositions of the 1790s, in which the figures are somewhat arbitrarily drawn. The location of this view, taken from the corner of Greenwich Park and hitherto unrecognized, is identified in a watercolour of the same scene (without the dragoons) which was with P. & D. Colnaghi in 1969.

29
**View in Windsor Forest, with oxen
drawing timber**

Bodycolour with some watercolour, over
touches of pencil, with black line surround;
$13\frac{1}{8} \times 18\frac{1}{8}$ (33·4 × 46)
Indistinctly signed and dated near bottom
left, *P Sandby 1793*; inscribed in ink in a
?contemporary hand on an old label
attached to the *verso*, *Scene in Winsor Forest –
Oxen dragging Timber/painted by Paul Sandby
R.A. in body colours on blue paper 1794/for Ann
Cobbe.*
415–1885
CONDITION: Fair, with some spotting
(?drops of oil) at centre
PROV: Anne Cobbe; purchased in 1885

A scene at the edge of the forest, with the
oxen and other figures in the foreground.
In the middle distance some horsemen are
pursuing deer on a grassy hillside, with, to
left, a lake beyond.
   A weak drawing, with the figures largely
out of scale; the attached inscription may
indicate that this was, at least partly, the
work of a pupil.

30
View of Rochester, Kent

Watercolour and bodycolour over pencil;
$19 \times 24\frac{7}{8}$ ($48 \cdot 2 \times 63 \cdot 2$)
Inscribed (?signed) in ink, at lower left, *P. Sandby R.A.*
D 1072–1904
CONDITION: Generally fair, except for discoloration at various places in the sky
PROV: James Orrock, R.I., by whom presented in 1904

The town dominated by the castle keep, is seen across the Medway in the centre, with the bridge, leading to further houses, at left: in the foreground a tree-lined meadow, with various figures, sheep and cattle.
    A drawing of the 1790s, with the common feature of considerable weaknesses and lack of scale in the figures. Paul Sandby exhibited two Rochester subjects at the RA in 1794 (Nos. 367 and 381). A very similar view of Rochester, somewhat smaller and with different figures in the foreground, is in the Whitworth Art Gallery, Manchester.

31
Roadway through Windsor Forest

Watercolour and pen and ink on white
paper, stuck down on thin board; $14\frac{3}{4} \times 21\frac{1}{8}$
$(37\cdot5 \times 55\cdot2)$
Inscribed, in pencil, at lower margin of the
old mount, *Portrait Windsor Forest Park
Sandby.*
Dyce 748
CONDITION: Good overall (after ?recent
cleaning), but with evidence of some tears
and folds, and with considerable rubbing,
particularly at lower right
PROV: William Dyce Bequest, 1869

The composition is dominated by a gnarled
and considerably damaged tree with two
main trunks; the road curves downhill to
right of this, with a man on horseback
riding up the hill and in the tree's shadow;
woodland beyond on left and a tree-lined
bank on right. It has been suggested that
the rider is 'probably intended for a
portrait of George III'.
   A bold and freely drawn composition
with harmonious colouring, dating from
the 1790s.

32
High Force, or Fall of the Tees, near Middleton High Tor

Watercolour with some scratching out, on white laid paper; $9\frac{1}{8} \times 11\frac{1}{8}$ (23 × 28·3)
1791–1900
CONDITION: Fair, with some darkening in the sky
PROV: Ashbee Bequest, 1900

The two cascades on either side of a wall of sheer rock are in the centre, falling into relatively calm water flowing to the left. There is more sheer rock on each side, with bushes and trees growing on it. In the foreground the river bank is strewn with rocks and stones.

   A somewhat weak drawing, probably dating from the late 1790s. High Force in Teesdale is considered one of the most impressive waterfalls in England, and has been described as 'a picturesque rocky cauldron, with a chaos of basaltic crags above'.

33
Bayswater Hill, London

Watercolour and some bodycolour over pencil, on white laid paper; 13 × 18⅞ (33 × 48)

Signed and dated in pen and ink on the back of the cart on right, *P S 1799*

D 1836–1904

CONDITION: Considerably rubbed and faded overall and yellowed in sky; some scuffs and a hole in foreground

PROV: Bequeathed by W. A. Sandby in 1904

EXH: ?RA 1800, No. 717; International Exhibitions Foundation, *British Watercolors from the Victoria and Albert Museum*, 1966–7, No. 79

A view up the hill with buildings among trees on left, and a park wall beneath trees on right; several groups of figures, including a coach coming down the hill and a cart with three horses going up it.

Another weak late drawing, with characteristically out-of-scale figures that are too small for their surroundings. Its pair may be the Museum of London's *Entrance to Bayswater Turnpike* (57.24), which could have been No. 710 at the 1800 RA Exhibition.

34
Windsor Castle: the North Terrace looking west, at sunset

Bodycolour on laminated laid paper; $14\frac{7}{8}$ × $21\frac{1}{8}$ (38×53) – irregular at upper margin
Signed and dated, in ink, on parapet at right, *P Sandby 1800*
D 1832–1904
CONDITION: Somewhat flattened and rubbed
PROV: Bequeathed by W. A. Sandby in 1904
EXH: Guildhall Art Gallery, *Paul Sandby*, 1960, No. 37; Reading and Bolton, *Thomas and Paul Sandby*, 1972, No. 72
LIT: M. Hardie, *Water-colour Painting in Britain*, Vol. 1, 1966, p. 106

The same view as in **10** and **14**, with rather fewer figures than in either: an evening scene with a pink-tinged sunset sky.

See also **10** and **14**. The soldier seated on the parapet at right margin is similar to a figure in a view of *Old Somerset House, the Garden or River front* in the Royal Collection (Oppé, No. 161), and must have been based on the same study, now lost. A comparison between the present drawing and **10** provides striking evidence of the deterioration in the quality of Sandby's gouaches during the three decades or so that separate them.

35
The Old Welsh Bridge, Shrewsbury

Bodycolour on canvas; 29 × 37 (73·7 × 94) –
sight 53–1887
CONDITION: There is considerable flaking in
the sky and elsewhere, and there are also
damp stains, etc.
PROV: Purchased in 1887 (Christie's,
19.3.1887, lot 39, £35)

A view of the bridge from the river, with
the gateway tower in the centre of the
composition; houses on the far bank at
right, and the castellated end pier in the
foreground at left. There are several boats
on the water, including, below the nearest
arch, a rowing boat with lady passengers
seated beneath a canopy in the stern, an
ensign fluttering behind them.

The Old Welsh Bridge over the River
Severn at Shrewsbury, which was replaced
in the 1790s, seems to have been a
favourite subject with Paul Sandby. He
produced an aquatint close in composition
to **35** in 1778, and exhibited a view of the
bridge at the RA in 1801. Drawings
comparable with the present composition
are in the British Museum (L. B. 35), at
Yale (B1976.7.143), and elsewhere. The
present version seems likely to have been
an exhibition piece, and dates from about
1800.

36
Moonlight on a river

Bodycolour on blue paper; $16\frac{5}{8} \times 23$ ($42 \cdot 2 \times 58 \cdot 4$) – sight
D 1839–1904
CONDITION: Good, except for some flaking in the sky
PROV: Bequeathed by W. A. Sandby in 1904
EXH: Guildhall Art Gallery, *Paul Sandby*, 1960, No. 14

A full moon among clouds is seen through trees growing on each side of the river. On the right bank is a small brick lodge with smoke rising from its chimney; in centre foreground the moon is reflected in the river, and to right a punt with two men on board is leaving the river bank. In the centre of the middle distance two men are watering their horses, and beyond are a church with a spire and other buildings.

A romantic composition which probably dates from about 1800.

37
Carreg-Cennen Castle,
Carmarthenshire

Bodycolour; $12\frac{1}{4} \times 18$ ($31 \times 45\cdot8$) – sight
D 1834–1904
(see also colour plate between pp. 64 and
65)
CONDITION: Good, with a few repairs in the
sky
PROV: Bequeathed by W. A. Sandby in
1904

The squat castle on its rocky prominence is
at centre, with rolling meadows below it
and in the foreground. At centre are three
women with a small haycart; more
haymakers at right. To the left is a group
of trees, and there are further trees
between the fields.

A late work of about 1800. Carreg
Cennen Castle is some $2\frac{1}{2}$ miles south-east
of Llandeilo, and remains today much as
shown by Sandby. There is a smaller
version or copy of this composition in the
British Art Center at Yale (Robertson
1985, 101).

Catalogue of watercolours and drawings by Thomas Sandby in the collection of the Victoria & Albert Museum

There is very little firm evidence on which
to date any but the earliest drawings by
Thomas Sandby. The small group
catalogued below is arranged in a tentative
chronological order, and an approximate
date is proposed for each sheet.

38

Windsor Castle from the Great Park, near the end of the Long Walk

Watercolour over pencil, on Whatman laid paper; $12\frac{3}{8} \times 19\frac{1}{2}$ ($31 \cdot 5 \times 49 \cdot 5$)
Inscribed in pencil on *verso* in an early nineteenth-century hand, *View of Windsor Castle/Paul Sandby* (last two words partly erased)
137-1892
(see also colour plate between pp. 64 and 65)
CONDITION: Slightly faded; one small damaged area in sky
PROV: Purchased in 1892
EXH: Reading and Bolton, *Thomas and Paul Sandby*, 1972 (No. 17)
LIT: *The Studio*, LXXII (1918), repr. p. 141, illustrating article on 'Paul and Thomas Sandby' by Frank Gibson; *The Connoisseur*, XCIII (1934), repr. in colour facing p. 340

The castle is seen in the middle distance to left of centre; in the left foreground a man and a woman are seated facing the castle on a bench beneath a single tree; to the right, groups of trees, with a herd of deer grazing among them and a couple walking in the foreground.

The attribution to Thomas Sandby is a long-standing one, and seems more tenable than one to Paul, despite the early inscription on the *verso*. The early 1750s would seem a likely date for this fine Windsor view, the composition of which is similar to that of *Windsor from the Lodge Grounds in the Great Park* at Windsor (RL 17751).

39
Park landscape, with house, Gothic ruin and ornamental water (probably Virginia Water)

Watercolour over pencil, on coarse white rag paper, stuck down on paper with a grey and yellow line-wash surround; $11\frac{1}{4} \times 20\frac{3}{4}$ (28.6×52.7) – original mount $13\frac{3}{8} \times 22\frac{5}{8}$ (34×57.5)
Inscribed in pencil at lower right, not in the artist's hand, *Thos. Sandby Architect.* There are various inventory and price inscriptions on the back of the mount
P 89-1937
CONDITION: Somewhat faded and rubbed
PROV: Basil S. Long, former Keeper of the Department of Paintings, by whom bequeathed in 1937

Paul Oppé (*Drawings of Paul and Thomas Sandby*, p. 43) stated that 'though possibly connected with Windsor Park', the present drawing 'cannot relate to Virginia Water' Recently the Hon. Mrs Jane Roberts has suggested in a letter to the compiler 'that the house must be the Wheatsheaf Hotel (cf. RL 17866), with a gothic ruin, of a type that recurs in the 'Clockcase' in the wrong place in the background'. The ornamental water, with its grotto and bridge, would thus be Virginia Water, but there is no sign of the cascade and there must continue to be some doubt as to the site of this drawing. However, it can be firmly attributed to Thomas Sandby, and must date from the mid-1750s, though, as has been proposed by Mrs Roberts in a paper delivered in 1984, 'in spite of repeated statements to the contrary, Thomas does *not* appear to have been the architect of the original lake and appurtenances', which were under construction around 1750, probably under the supervision of Henry Flitcroft (1697–1769). The grotto in **39** is similar to that seen in drawings at Yale (Robertson, 1958, 21), San Francisco, Bolton and elsewhere, and also in the fourth of the 1754 set of engravings of *Eight Views of Windsor Great Park.*

40
**Design for a gateway at Windsor Park
in the form of a triumphal arch**

Pen and ink and wash, over pencil, on laid
paper; $6\frac{1}{2} \times 7\frac{3}{8}$ ($16\cdot5 \times 18\cdot7$) – both top
corners cut off
Inscribed in pencil at lower margin, *In
Windsor Park – design for Windsor – T Sandby
RA;* partly in the artist's hand
3436-177
CONDITION: Somewhat dirty overall, and
torn at right margin and corners
PROV: C. J. Richardson Collection,
purchased 1863

A view from slightly to the left of a large
ornamental stone gateway in classical style
and in the form of a triumphal arch. The
central wooden panelled double gate is set
into an arch between pairs of Corinthian
columns under an ornate cornice, above
which is a low stone structure with square
columns at each corner and an inscribed
panel in the centre. There are lower single
wooden gates to left and right, set in
rusticated masonry terminating in massive
Tuscan columns.

There is no record of such a classical
gateway at Windsor. The drawing
probably dates from the 1760s.

41
Design for a gateway at Windsor Castle in the form of a triumphal arch

Pen and ink and watercolour on white cartridge paper; $25 \times 27\frac{3}{4}$ ($63\cdot5 \times 70\cdot5$)
Inscribed in pencil at lower left, *Sandby the Archt Design for Gateway Windsor Castle*
2827
CONDITION: Faded and rubbed with several old folds, and numerous tears at the margins
PROV: Purchased in 1863

A much more finished frontal view, drawn with the aid of a ruler, of the same gateway as that in **40**. The major variation is that in the present drawing the wooden gates fill the entire arch in each case, while in **40** a semicircular opening is shown above each gate.

It is possible that this highly finished drawing was executed to illustrate a lecture, and thus it would date from about 1770.

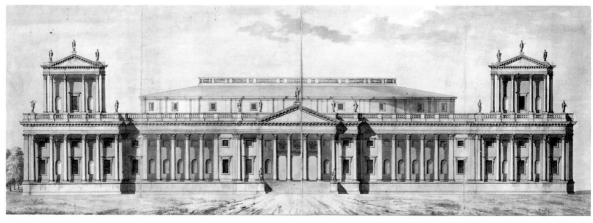

42

Design for a National Mausoleum or Temple of Fame

Watercolour and pen and ink (using ruler and compass) on laid paper, stuck down on cartridge paper; $17\frac{1}{4} \times 49\frac{7}{8}$ ($43 \cdot 8 \times 126 \cdot 8$) Inscribed in pencil at bottom of backing paper, *Professor of Architecture at the Royal Academy – Thomas Sandby 1721–1798 – A Design for a National Moseleum* [sic] *or Temple of Fame* D 2007-1885 (see also colour plate between pp. 64 and 65) CONDITION: Existing fold at centre and former folds at centre of left and right halves; several tears and holes crudely repaired. The overall condition is relatively crisp with well-preserved colours PROV: Purchased in 1885

A frontal view of a wide classical façade largely on two floors, with Corinthian columns across its entire length, supporting an entablature with a balustrade above. At the centre, the entrance beneath a pediment is supported by six columns. At the left and right ends the façade projects slightly and there are pedimented pavilions, each with four columns, above. At the main points of these, as above the entrance, are classical statues. Behind the façade, and extending along its centre, are seen the upper storey, roof and balustrade of the rear portion of the building.

This powerful and imaginative design was probably executed as an illustration for a lecture in the 1770s.

43

Design for the elevation of a prison

Watercolour and pen and ink (using a
ruler), on laid paper; $11\frac{5}{8} \times 32\frac{3}{8}$ ($29 \cdot 5 \times 82 \cdot 3$)
3436–180

CONDITION: On the whole good, but with
some long tears well repaired. The paper is
joined and was formerly folded along the
centre, and there is crude retouching and
repair in this area. Rather dirty in sky and
at margins.

PROV: C. J. Richardson Collection;
purchased in 1863

A symmetrical façade on two floors in an
overall rusticated stone finish with some
polished masonry details. In the centre four
wide steps lead to an entrance set between
pairs of circular semi-rusticated attached
columns supporting a plain pediment.
There are four windows on each floor to
left and right, with pairs of rectangular
semi-rusticated attached columns at each
end of the building. The low pitched roof
is surrounded by a plain masonry wall,
with a cornice below.

While the attribution to Thomas Sandby
is entirely plausible, the suggestion that this
was a design for Newgate Prison cannot be
supported. That prison was erected in
1770–8 to designs by George Dance; it
bore no resemblance to the present
drawing and was demolished in 1802. Like
the preceding sheet, **43** may have been
executed as an illustration to a lecture and
can be dated to the 1770s.

44

Strawberry Hill: Interior of the Gallery

Pen and ink and watercolour, on laid paper stuck down on thin board with grey line-wash border; $21\frac{3}{8} \times 29\frac{3}{8}$ (54×75) – $23 \times 31\frac{1}{2}$ (58.4×80) to edges of mount.
Inscribed in ink at centre of lower margin of the old mount, *Gallery at Strawberry Hill*, and at lower right, *T. Sandby. P. Sandby & E. Edwards 1781*; and, in ink, on the *verso* of the old mount, *I give this drawing by Thomas Sandby to the Victoria and Albert Museum/at South Kensington, for Exhibition there./Feb 1904 W. Sandby*. There are three further inscriptions by William Sandby in ink on two labels formerly attached to the old frame; *This drawing is mentioned by Horace Walpole in a letter to the Rev W. Cole, dated 16 June, 1781. Purchased at Christie's from Lord Waldegrave's Sale of Strawberry Hill Collection. Feb. 1900 W.S.*; and '*A painter is to come here on Monday to . . . finish T. Sandby's fine view of the Gallery, to which I could never get him to put the last hand.*' (See *Horace Walpole's Correspondence*, ed. W. S. Lewis, Vol. 2, 1937, p. 274); and *Ed. Edwards A.R.A. a friend of T.S. who filled in the upper portrait at the right hand. The whole of the rest is by T.S.*
D 1837-1904
CONDITION: Much faded and rubbed; fold in centre
PROV: 9th Earl of Waldegrave (descendant of Horace Walpole), sold Christie's, February 1900; William Sandby; bequeathed by him in 1904 (specifically allocated to South Kensington by him)
EXH: R.A., 1782, No. 241; Twickenham, Orleans House Gallery, *Horace Walpole and Strawberry Hill*, 1980, No. 126
LIT: Horace Walpole, *A Description of the Villa . . . at Strawberry-Hill . . .*, 1784, small engraving by T. Morris facing p. 47; W. S. Lewis, *Horace Walpole*, 1961, repr. pl. 37

A view down the Gallery with the windows on the left; very detailed rendering of the ornate ceiling, panelling, carpet, furniture, paintings, sculpture, etc. The three-quarter length female portrait at right margin is clearly by a different hand (see inscription).

The interior of the Gallery was under construction from 1761 to 1763, apparently inspired by the gallery at Chantilly. The ornate canopied niches and doors were imitated from the tomb of Archbishop Bourchier (*d.* 1486) near the altar of Canterbury Cathedral. On 24 June 1770, Horace Walpole wrote to Paul Sandby asking him to remind his brother Thomas that he had promised to come and draw the Gallery (*Horace Walpole's Correspondence*, ed. W. S. Lewis, Vol. 41, 1980, p. 189). The letter written to the Rev. W. Cole eleven years later, and quoted in one of the inscriptions cited above, indicates that Thomas Sandby never completed this ambitious drawing. W. T. Whitley (*Artists and their Friends in England, 1700-1799*, 1928, Vol. 2, p. 395) cites the following quotation from Horace Walpole's RA Catalogue notes; 'T. Sandby drew this by the eye in two days and a half. His brother Paul put in the pictures and Mr. Edwards painted the carpets, chairs and table.' Under the circumstances it appears surprising that Thomas Sandby chose to exhibit this drawing at the Royal Academy. Edward Edwards (1736-1806), who is best known for his *Anecdotes of Painters*, 1808, was a friend of both Sandbys. His association with Paul is discussed below in the entry for **52g**. During the last two years of Thomas's life, when he himself was too ill to deliver his RA lectures, these were read for him by Edwards.

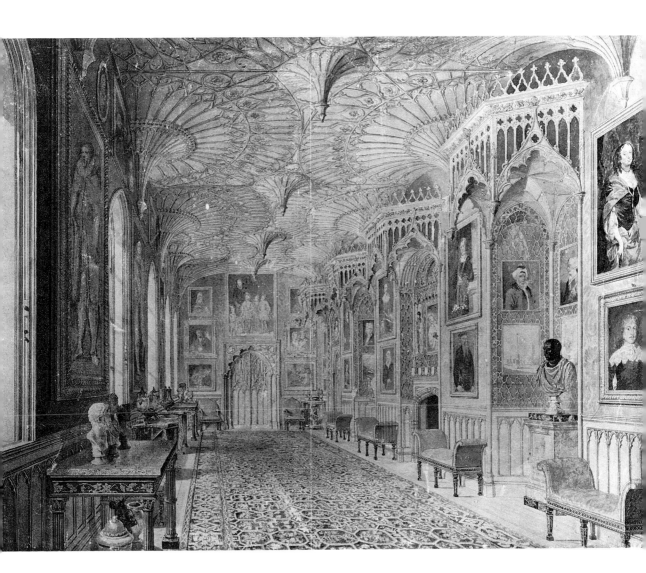

45

Design for a bridge at Somerset House; view across the bridge

Watercolour over pencil (using ruler and compass), on white laid paper; $17\frac{1}{2} \times 14\frac{1}{4}$ (44·5 × 36·2)
D 1840-1904
CONDITION: Fair, with some rubbing and creasing
PROV: William Sandby, by whom bequeathed in 1904
EXH: ?R.A., 1781, No. 462

A diagonal view from within the imposing entrance Pavilion, with Ionic columns, coffered ceiling, and large sash windows, towards the domed exit at the other end, to the left.

For a discussion of this and the other 'Bridge of Magnificence' drawings, see the note to **47** below. A second view across the bridge in the V & A (D 1400-98) is very feebly drawn and is probably a copy after Thomas Sandby, and cannot be attributed to that artist himself.

46

Design for a bridge at Somerset House; view looking east

Pen and ink and watercolour, over pencil; $9\frac{7}{8} \times 24\frac{3}{8}$ (25·1 × 61·9)
Inscribed in ink, on the back of the old mount, *Design for a bridge over the Thames at Somerset House. By Thos Sandby*
D 822-1899
CONDITION: Somewhat faded overall; various crudely repaired tears, especially at the right margin
PROV: Purchased in 1899 (R. Jackson, £1. 15. 0)
EXH: Barbican Gallery, *London in Perspective*, 1984, No. 6

In the left foreground the river front of the Adelphi is seen, at the end of which is the northern entrance pavilion of the seven-arched bridge, of which five arches and the central pavilion are shown. Somerset House, St Paul's Cathedral and Blackfriars Bridge are seen through the arches. In the foreground are moored and moving boats.

For a discussion of this drawing see the note to **47** below.

47

Design for a bridge at Somerset House; view looking west

Pen and ink and watercolour, over pencil; $10\frac{3}{4} \times 46\frac{5}{8}$ ($27 \cdot 3 \times 118 \cdot 5$)
Inscribed in pen at lower left, *T. Sandby*
D 1363–1898
CONDITION: Dirty and faded overall; paper joined in right half
PROV: Purchased in 1898 (R. Jackson, £3)
EXH: Reading and Bolton, *Thomas and Paul Sandby*, 1972, No. 7

The river front of Somerset House is seen in the right foreground, with the northern domed pavilion of the bridge adjoining it at the left. The whole of the nine-arched bridge is seen crossing the river to the left. There is a 'Palladian' central pavilion, and a second domed pavilion at the south end.

Nos **45-47** belong to the group of about forty drawings which Thomas Sandby executed as illustrations for the sixth and final lecture of his annual series which he delivered as Professor of Architecture at the Royal Academy. He is said to have repeated these lectures annually from 1770 until his death in 1798, though in the final two years they were read for him by Edward Edwards, ARA, who had been appointed Professor of Perspective in 1788. Sandby exhibited two of these drawings at the RA in 1781 (Nos 450 and 462). Other drawings from this series are at Windsor, the British Museum, the Royal Institute of British Architects, and elsewhere. The manuscript of Sandby's lecture is at the RIBA (there is another copy at Sir John Soane's Museum), but the drawings were dispersed in the sale held after Thomas Sandby's death.

It seems improbable that these drawings associated with the Bridge of Magnificence across the Thames close to Somerset House could have been used for the earlier lectures, for William Chambers's new Somerset House was being built between 1776 and 1786, and in several of the drawings, including **47**, the river front is shown almost complete. Therefore these drawings cannot date from earlier than

about 1780, and even then Sandby would have had to have had access to Chambers's designs, which was certainly possible as the two architects were on friendly terms. The RIBA manuscript (SaT/1/1–2) is Thomas Sandby's own copy of his lectures, and the text has been much altered and amended by Sandby himself and by others. In the case of the sixth lecture it seems certain that much of it must post-date 1770 by some years; this definitely applies to the descriptions of the drawings of the Ornamental Bridge, of which it is stated (pp. 49–50):

> This design was not made with any Idea of its being carried into execution. It was composed on purpose for this lecture, to shew in what manner the River Thames might be further usefully adorned by opening another communication between this great Commercial City and its suburbs. The situation best calculated for such a Design would be between Westminster and Blackfriars Bridges, where the approach to it would be easy and commodious, such as the elevated situation of the Strand, near Exeter Change. On this Idea I formed the design, where it would in some measure, assimilate and unite with the new and elegant Pile of Building now carrying on at Somerset Place, where its extensive and noble Terrace would terminate with the central arch of the Pavilion over the abutment of that end of the Bridge, and where the passage over it would be on a level with the Strand.

Again it may be concluded that Sandby's designs for the bridge must date from about 1780. Further evidence of Thomas Sandby's interest in the building of New Somerset House is to be found in two impressive drawings of it under construction, which are included in Vol. VI of J. C. Crowle's extra-illustrated copy of Pennant's *London* in the British Museum (L. B., 20 and 22).

The classical design of Sandby's bridge was inspired by G. B. Piranesi's print of a Triumphal Bridge, published in *Prima Parte di Architetture e Prospettive* in 1743. One of Sandby's royal patrons, William Henry, Duke of Gloucester, younger brother of George III, had given the architect a magnificent fifteen-volume set of Piranesi's *Works*, soon after he himself had received it at an audience with the Pope on a visit to Rome, either in 1771 or early in 1776. The obituary of Thomas Sandby in *The Gentleman's Magazine* (July 1798, p. 630) mentions that 'one of his latest plans was a noble design for a bridge across the Thames at Somerset House', which indicates again that these drawings must date from the later years of his life. The right half of the bridge is reproduced in aquatint in Vol. II of Samuel Ireland's *Picturesque Views on the River Thames*, 1791 (facing p. 187). The first Waterloo Bridge was opened on Sandby's site in 1817.

48
**Design for a rock-work structure on
the bank of a lake**

Watercolour and pen and ink on laid
paper; $13\frac{1}{4} \times 19\frac{3}{8}$ ($33\cdot6 \times 49\cdot2$)
Inscribed in pencil, in a later hand, at
lower right. *By Sandby the Archt./for Windsor
Park*
3436–172
CONDITION: Good
PROV: C. J. Richardson Collection;
purchased in 1863

The very irregular rock-work structure,
overgrown with bushes, is seen at the edge
of the water in the middle distance, with
parkland and trees beyond. In the
foreground, as if on a spit of grass, is the
ground-plan of the structure, annotated
with measurements.

For a discussion of this and the following
two Virginia Water designs see the note to
50 below.

49
Design for a rock-work folly

Watercolour and pen and ink on laid
paper; $9\frac{1}{2} \times 16\frac{5}{8}$ ($24\cdot2 \times 42\cdot3$)
Inscribed in pencil, in a later hand, at
lower right. *By Sandby the Archt./for Windsor
Park*
3436–173
CONDITION: Good, the paper somewhat
darkened
PROV: C. J. Richardson Collection;
purchased in 1863

A circular 'rock-temple' on two levels with
several cavernous openings, and trees and
bushes growing on top. Beyond, a bare
hillside; the sky and foreground are
indicated.
See note to **50** below.

50
Design for a rock-work bridge

Watercolour and pen and ink, on laid
paper; $7\frac{5}{8} \times 17$ ($19\cdot4 \times 43\cdot2$)
Inscribed in pencil, in a later hand, at
lower right. *Sandby Archt/1805*
3436-174
CONDITION: Good, the paper somewhat
darkened
PROV: C. J. Richardson Collection;
purchased in 1863

A small bridge with one semicircular arch
constructed of yellowish rocks is seen in
elevation, with rocks and grass to left and
right. There is no indication of what the
bridge crosses, or of sky, etc.

No. **50** and the preceding two drawings
of rock-work structures belong to the large
number of surviving sheets associated with
Thomas Sandby's work at Virginia Water,
of which there are groups in the collections
at Windsor, the Bodleian Library (Gough
Collection), and elsewhere. It has always
been thought that Thomas Sandby was
associated with the Duke of Cumberland's
original work in the creation of Virginia
Water around 1750. However, in her
unpublished paper 'The Sandby Brothers
at Windsor', the Hon. Jane Roberts has
suggested that it was Henry Flitcroft who
made the original designs for Virginia
Water, and that it was only after damage
caused by serious floods in 1768 and 1782
that Thomas Sandby was responsible for
the enlargement of the lake and the
building of a new cascade and grotto.
Thomas Sandby's original patron at
Windsor, William, Duke of Cumberland,
died in 1765, and it was his nephew,
Henry Frederick, fourth son of Frederick,
Prince of Wales (who succeeded as Ranger
of Windsor Forest, and was then created
Duke of Cumberland on attaining his
majority in 1766) who commissioned
Thomas Sandby's work at Virginia Water.
At present there is no information as to the
commencement and duration of this work,
but it seems probable that much of this
must have occurred in the 1780s, and it is
feasible to date these drawings to this
decade. See also the note to **39** above.

51
**Design for a gateway or bridge in
imitation of Gothick ruins**

Watercolour with pen and ink, on rag
paper; $4\frac{1}{2} \times 8\frac{11}{16}$ ($11\cdot5 \times 22\cdot2$)
Inscribed in pencil at lower right, *T.
Sandby*, and with indecipherable words in
upper margin. On the *verso* there are
various pencil doodles of rocks, etc. At
lower right of the old backing paper, in
pencil, *Sandby Archt. For Windsor Park.*
3436–179
CONDITION: Slightly faded, dirty and scuffed
PROV: C. J. Richardson Collection;
purchased in 1863

In the centre is a low arched castellated
gateway, with partly ruinous two-storeyed
buildings adjoining it to left and right.
There are trees and bushes in front of and
behind the building at both left and right.
A roadway leads up to the gateway in the
centre.

There are some similarities between this
design and Thomas Sandby's much larger
designs for a Gothic arch and bridge in the
Royal Library (Oppé, Nos. 122, 123, 124
and S. 433). It appears that no such
structure was erected at Virginia Water or
elsewhere in Windsor Park during Thomas
Sandby's lifetime. In style and technique
51 resembles the rock-work drawings, and
a date in the 1780s also seems appropriate
here.

Catalogue of watercolours and drawings in the Carr Album, by, and attributed to, Paul and Thomas Sandby

52

D 92–290–1901

In 1901 Mrs Jane Carr bequeathed an album containing 199 drawings and 2 engravings by, and attributed to, Paul and Thomas Sandby. The album was subsequently broken up, and the drawings were arranged on mounts, with up to eleven drawings on each. It is impracticable to include a catalogue of all these drawings here, and only a selection is reproduced and catalogued below. Among these are some drawings which are of considerable interest in the study of the work of the Sandbys.

Mrs Carr was the daughter of a Mr Alnutt and the widow of Henry Carr. An elderly lady at the time of her death, she is said to have been a pupil of David Cox. There is no record of any connection with the Sandby family, or of how the album was acquired. While the attribution of a few of the drawings to either brother is doubtful, many of them are inscribed with the *F* mark which is found on numerous pencil or chalk drawings by the Sandbys. This mark, which is discussed by Paul Oppé on p. 20 of his book on the *Sandby drawings at Windsor Castle*, has yet to be convincingly interpreted. (See also the note to **8** above.)

The largest categories of drawings in the Carr Album are as follows:

Scottish figure studies by Paul Sandby
Other figure and animal studies by Paul Sandby
Architectural studies by Thomas Sandby
Decorative studies by Thomas Sandby

There are also various types of drawings by both brothers which do not fit into any of these categories. Each drawing catalogued and illustrated below is separately numbered, **52a** etc.; the drawings by Paul precede those by Thomas.

PAUL SANDBY

52a

A group of ten standing men in hats and coats

Pen and ink and watercolour; $2\frac{1}{2} \times 6$ ($6\cdot3 \times 15\cdot2$)

D 216–1901

The Carr Album includes some 25 such Scottish figure studies, of which there are further examples at Windsor, the British Museum and in other collections. They are thought to be on-the-spot studies executed in Edinburgh and elsewhere during Sandby's years in Scotland, from 1747 to 1750.

52b
**Three men working on a block of
stone in a quarry**

Pencil and watercolour; $4 \times 4\frac{7}{8}$ ($10 \cdot 1 \times 12 \cdot 4$)
D 203–1901

This may be a preliminary sketch for *Road
builders shifting boulders* in the National
Gallery of Scotland (*The Discovery of
Scotland*, 1978, No. 4.5), and is certainly a
drawing of about 1750.

52c
**Interior with a young man seated by a
fireside**

Pencil; $4\frac{5}{8} \times 5\frac{1}{4}$ ($11 \cdot 7 \times 13 \cdot 4$)
Inscribed at centre of lower margin, in
pencil, *F*
D 189–1901

A freely-drawn study of *c.* 1760.

52d
Two four-wheeled carriages, with horses harnessed to them

Pencil; $2\frac{1}{4} \times 5$ ($5 \cdot 7 \times 12 \cdot 7$)
Inscribed at centre of lower margin, in pencil, *F*
D 134–1901

A rapid and effective drawing of *c*. 1760.

52e
An orientalised circular building, set among trees in an ornamental garden

Pencil; $5\frac{1}{8} \times 4\frac{1}{2}$ ($13 \times 11 \cdot 5$)
Inscribed at centre of lower margin, in pencil, *F*, and at right, *Mr. Whitbreads Bath at Bed*[*well*]

Samuel Whitbread the Elder bought Bedwell Park, Little Berkhampsted, Hertfordshire, in 1765. There is no known connection between the Sandbys and the Whitbreads. The present drawing is an effective rapid on-the-spot study dating from about 1770.

52f
A lady walking between a boy and a girl

Pen and ink and grey wash; $3\frac{1}{8} \times 1\frac{5}{8}$ ($8 \times 4\cdot1$)
D130–1901

This group appears, the same size, under one of the arches of the arcade to the left of the large watercolour *The Piazza, Covent Garden* by Thomas Sandby at the British Museum (L. B. 18; *British Landscape Watercolours*, 1985, No. 14, pl. 9), which is thought to date from the mid-1760s.

52g
A muse emblematic of drawing, with a cherub showing her an Egyptian figurine

Pen and ink and grey wash; $2\frac{1}{2} \times 3\frac{1}{4}$ ($6\cdot3 \times 8\cdot3$)
Inscribed at upper left, in pencil, *E. Edwards*, and above this *F*
D183–1901

Presumably a design for a trade card or the like for the artist Edward Edwards, ARA (1738–1806), who was appointed Professor of Perspective at the Royal Academy in 1788, and who was a friend of both the Sandbys. Edward's own *Collection of Views and Studies after Nature with Other Subjects*, published in 1790, includes several etchings of somewhat similar emblematic figure compositions, and the central figure of the etching included as the frontispiece of his *A Practical Treatise of Perspective*, 1803, is also similar in subject and character.

52h
Archibald Robertson's shop in Savill Row Passage with Squibbs Auction Room beyond

Pen and ink and grey wash; $2\frac{5}{8} \times 3\frac{7}{8}$ (6·7 × 9·2),
D 182–1901

This is the design for the head-piece of Archibald Robertson's trade-card, in which he describes himself as 'Print-Seller and Drawing-Master in Savill Row Passage, adjoining Squibbs Auction Room', and advertises a variety of materials for drawing and print-making, the engraving of visiting cards, framing and glazing, etc. He also states: 'Sandby's works in Aqua Tinta to be had complete'. Little is known about Archibald Robertson, who was active in London from 1765 to 1796. He exhibited at the Royal Academy between 1772 and 1796, and in 1775 gave Savill Row Passage as his address in the catalogue. Paul Sandby's aquatint series were published in the later 1770s, and include a series of Italian views, mostly after Pietro Fabris, published in partnership with Archibald Robertson in 1777.

52i
Bearers and pall-bearers carrying the coffin at a spinster's funeral

Pencil, $3\frac{5}{8} \times 6$ (9·2 × 15·3)
D 192–1901

This sensitive study relates to the group carrying a coffin to the door of the church in *The West Front of St. Paul's, Covent Garden*, engraved by E. Rooker after Paul Sandby, and published by John Boydell on 1 January 1777. The compiler owes the identification of this as a spinster's funeral to Julian Litten of the Victoria and Albert Museum.

52j
A crowd around a gibbet with two corpses hanging from it

Pencil; $6 \times 4\frac{3}{8}$ ($15 \cdot 2 \times 11 \cdot 1$)
D 197-1901
A rapid sketch of the 1770s. Another drawing in the Carr Album (D 141) shows just the gibbet with the corpses hanging from it.

52k
A girl carrying a tray near a fence, with a pair of wooden steps and a laundry basket in the foreground

Pencil and pen and ink; $4\frac{5}{8} \times 3\frac{3}{4}$ ($11 \cdot 8 \times 9 \cdot 5$)
– there are two large blood stains at right and bottom left of the sheet
D 188-1901

521

A girl descending steps, carrying a tray; behind her a wall with an urn on top and a carved relief with four figures below this

Pencil with some pen and ink; $7\frac{1}{8} \times 4\frac{1}{4}$ (18.1×10.8)
D 175-1901

52m

An archway leading to an entrance hall; a female bust on a plinth to left, an open doorway to right

Pencil; $4 \times 6\frac{3}{8}$ (10.2×16.2)
Inscribed at lower right, in pencil, F
D 196-1901

This and the two preceding drawings (**52k** and **52l**) are all presumably on-the-spot studies made in the courtyard of Paul Sandby's studio at 4 St George's Row, Bayswater, to which he had moved in 1772 and where he lived until his death. Later known as 23 Hyde Park Place, the house was demolished in 1901. The three scenes are repeated with variations and on a smaller scale in Paul Sandby's overall view of his studio and the courtyard in the British Museum (L.B. 19; repr. here as Fig. 13). Another smaller and weaker bodycolour version of this composition, with different figures, is in the Castle Museum at Nottingham (45-159). **Nos. 52k** to **m** show Paul Sandby's draughtsmanship of the 1770s at its freest and most fluent.

52n
A triumphal arch, surmounted by a monument of a horseman, in an Italianate landscape setting

Watercolour and pen and ink; $4\frac{1}{2} \times 6\frac{1}{2}$
($11\cdot5 \times 16\cdot5$)
D 185–1901

A forceful drawing of *c.* 1780.

52o
An extensive mess-tent near trees

Pen and ink and grey wash; $3\frac{1}{4} \times 8\frac{3}{4}$ ($8\cdot4 \times 22\cdot2$)
D 170–1901

Probably drawn at one of the 1780 encampments in Hyde Park and other London parks of troops assembled on account of the Gordon Riots. Paul Sandby made numerous drawings of and at these encampments, and they were also the subject of two sets of aquatints. The Carr Album includes several other small studies of encampment scenes.

Thomas Sandby

52p
Scene in the park of a Continental château

Pen and ink and grey wash; $7\frac{5}{8} \times 6\frac{3}{8}$ (19·4 × 16·3)
D 180–1901

The discovery in the British Museum of a signed and dated etching of the same composition, with only small variations in details, confirms the unlikely attribution of this very French drawing to Thomas Sandby. The etching, which is reversed and marginally larger and more finished than the drawing, is inscribed at lower left, *Thos Sandby Sculp 1741* (the first six letters etched, the rest in ink). It was purchased by the BM from J. Deffet Francis in 1867 (1867-12-14-479). A second drawing in the Carr Album (D 178-1901), which shows a grand staircase leading to a classical building, has similarities in style and subject matter to the present drawing, and may also be an unexpected early work by Thomas Sandby.

52q
Lichtenbergh

Pen and ink, with grey wash and some pencil; $3\frac{1}{8} \times 6\frac{1}{8}$ ($8 \times 16 \cdot 3$)
Inscribed across the sky, in pencil, *Lichtenbergh*
D 262–1901

This would appear to be a copy after Wenceslaus Hollar (1607–1677), though no drawing or print of Lichtenbergh by him has been traced. Only its presence in the Carr Album lends credence to a possible attribution to Thomas or Paul Sandby. There are several Lichtenberghs in Germany, including one on the River Mulde near Dresden.

52r
The nave of a Gothic church

Pen and ink and grey wash; $5\frac{1}{8} \times 4\frac{1}{2}$ ($13 \times 11 \cdot 5$)

A competent freehand architectural drawing, plausibly considered to be an early work of Thomas Sandby.

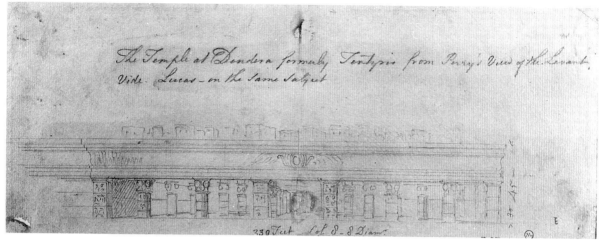

52s
Sketch of part of the Temple at Denderah, Egypt

Pencil; $4\frac{3}{8} \times 12\frac{3}{8}$ ($12 \times 31 \cdot 5$)
Inscribed, in pencil in the artist's hand, at upper margin, *The Temple at Dendera formerly Tentyra from Parry's View of the Levant vide Lucas – on the same subject*, and, at lower margin, with measurements and *F*
D 259–1901

The temple dates from the Ptolemaic period and was a favourite with European travellers and artists. A large drawing of Denderah by Thomas is at Yale.

52t
The façade of a Palladian villa

Pencil; $2\frac{3}{8} \times 3\frac{1}{4}$ ($6 \times 8 \cdot 3$)
Inscribed at lower right, in pencil, *F*
D 251–1901

52u
The façade of 'Chiswick House'

Pencil; $2\frac{7}{8} \times 3\frac{1}{4}$ ($7 \cdot 3 \times 8 \cdot 3$)
Inscribed, in pencil, at upper margin, *Chiswick House*, and at upper right, *F*
D 257–1901

This sketch has always been thought to represent Lord Burlington's Chiswick Villa, but it differs considerably from this in many details. It could represent the earlier house, demolished in 1788, to which Lord Burlington added his villa, though it appears rather like an amalgamation of the two.

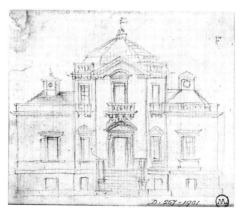

D. 290-1901.

Mr. Wilson presents best Compts. to Mr. Sandby, hopes he will accept many Thanks for the two elegant Designs he was so good as to give Col: Deakin for Mr. Wilson, who finds himself under the disagreeable Necessity, from the Stupidity of the Workmen at Normanby, to request the Favor of Mr. Sandby to give such a vertical Section of the above Design as will enable the Carpenter to execute it. The Carpenter does not know how to frame the inside or what scantlings the pieces should be that compose it.

52v
Design for a clock tower with Doric columns and a dome

Pen and ink and grey wash; $11\frac{3}{4} \times 6\frac{1}{4}$ (29·8 × 15·8) – irregular
Inscribed in ink, underneath the design.
Mr. Wilson presents best Compts. to Mr. Sandby, hopes he will accept/many Thanks for the two elegant designs he was so good as to give/ Col: Deakin for Mr. Wilson, who finds himself under the disagreeable Necessi/ty, from the stupidity of the workmen at Normanby, to request the/Favor of Mr. Sandby to give such a vertical Section of the above/Design as will enable the Carpenter to execute it. The/Carpenter does not know how to frame the inside or what/scantlings the pieces should be that compose it.
D 290-1901

Thomas Sandby designed Holly Grove, near Windsor, for Colonel Deacon (see drawing at BM, L. B. 27 (2), and H.M. Colvin, *Biographical Dictionary of British Architects, 1600–1840*, p. 522). There is no known connection between Sandby and Normanby Park in Lincolnshire.

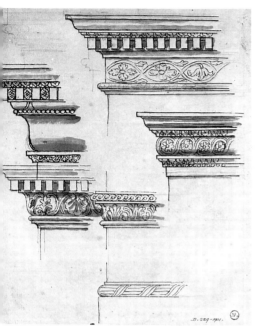

52w
Several studies of cornices

Pen and ink over pencil; $6\frac{1}{2} \times 6$ (16·5 × 15·2)
D 229–1901

52x
Detailed study of a capital, frieze with Masonic symbols, and cornice, in neo-classical style

Pen and ink and grey wash, over pencil; $9\frac{3}{8} \times 6\frac{3}{8}$ (23·8 × 16·2)
Inscribed in pencil, at upper margin, *Free Masons Hall*
D 226–1901

This and the preceding drawing, and also a few further drawings in the Carr Album, are connected with Thomas Sandby's most important executed work, the Freemasons' Hall in Queen Street, Lincoln's Inn Fields, which was built in 1775–6, and demolished in 1932.

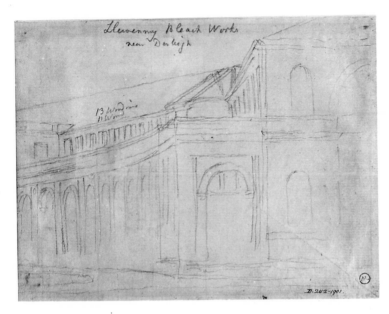

52y
Sketch of the Llewenny Bleach Works near Denbigh

Pencil; $4\frac{7}{8} \times 6\frac{1}{2}$ ($12\cdot4 \times 16\cdot5$)
Inscribed at lower margin, in pencil, *F*,
and at upper margin, *Llewenny Bleach Works near Denbigh*, and on the roof, *13 Windows 11 Wind*
D 242–1901

Thomas Sandby designed the bleach works near Denbigh for the Hon. Thomas Fitzmaurice in about 1785.

Select bibliography and abbreviations

Reference to the very few manuscript sources available are given in the notes to the Introduction, and in the relevant catalogue entries. Printed sources – books, articles and exhibition catalogues – are listed here in the alphabetical order of the authors' names. Where abbreviations are used in references to publications cited in the text or catalogue, these are given at the end of the appropriate bibliography entry below.

BALL, Johnson, *Paul and Thomas Sandby, Royal Academicians. An Anglo-Danish Saga of Art, Love and War in Georgian England*, Cheddar, Somerset, 1985. (Ball, 1985)

BINYON, Laurence, *Catalogue of Drawings by British Artists ... in the British Museum*, IV, London, 1907. (L. B.)

CROFT-MURRAY, Edward, *Decorative Painting in England, 1537–1837*, Vol. Two: *The Eighteenth and Early Nineteenth Centuries*, London, 1970.

FAIGAN, Julian, *Paul Sandby Drawings*, Australian Gallery Directors' Council, Sydney, 1981.

FARINGTON, Joseph, *The Diary of Joseph Farington*, ed. Kenneth Garlick, Angus Macintyre, and Kathryn Cave, I–XVI, New Haven and London, 1978–84.

GANDON, James, *The Life of James Gandon, Esq., ...* ed. Thomas J. Mulvany, Dublin, 1846; reprint London, 1969. (Gandon)

GRAVES, Algernon, *The Royal Academy of Arts: A Complete Dictionary of Contributors and their work ...*, Vol. VII, London, 1906; reprint London, 1970.

GUILDHALL ART GALLERY, *Paul Sandby, 1725–1809*, Foreword by J. L. Howgego, London, 1960.

HARDIE, Martin, *Water-colour Painting in Britain*, Vol. 1. *The Eighteenth Century*, ed. by Dudley Snelgrove, with Jonathan Mayne and Basil Taylor, London, 1966.

HERRMANN, Luke, 'Paul Sandby in Scotland', *Burlington Magazine*, CVI (1964), pp. 339–43.

HERRMANN, Luke, 'Paul Sandby in Scotland: A Sketch-book', *Burlington Magazine*, CVII (1965), pp. 467–8.

HERRMANN, Luke, *British Landscape Painting of the Eighteenth Century*, London and New York, 1973.

HUGHES, Peter, 'Paul Sandby and Sir Watkin Williams-Wynn', *Burlington Magazine*, CXIV (1972), pp. 459–66.

HUGHES, Peter, 'Paul Sandby's Tour of Wales with Joseph Banks', *Burlington Magazine*, CXVII (1975), pp. 452–7.

HUTCHISON, Sidney C., *The History of the Royal Academy, 1768–1968*, London, 1968.

NOTTINGHAM ART MUSEUM, Nottingham Castle, *Catalogue of the Special Exhibition ... of Drawings and Pictures by Thomas Sandby, R.A., and Paul Sandby, R.A.*, Nottingham, 1884.

OPPÉ, Paul, 'The Memoir of Paul Sandby by his Son', *Burlington Magazine*, LXXXVIII (1947), pp. 143-7. (Oppé, *Burlington*)

OPPÉ, Paul, *The Drawings of Paul and Thomas Sandby in the Collection of His Majesty The King at Windsor Castle*, Oxford and London, 1947. (Oppé, 1947)

OPPÉ, Paul, *English Drawings – Stuart and Georgian Periods – in the Collection of His Majesty The King at Windsor Castle*, London, 1950. (Oppé, 1950)

PAULSON, Ronald, *Hogarth: His Life, Art, and Times*, 2 Vols., New Haven, 1971.

RAMSDEN, E. H., 'The Sandby Brothers in London', *Burlington Magazine*, LXXXVIII (1947), pp. 15-18.

READING ART GALLERY (also shown at Bolton Museum and Art Gallery), *Thomas and Paul Sandby*, Reading, 1972.

ROBERTSON, Bruce, 'In at the Birth of British Historical Landscape Painting', *Turner Studies*, 4 (1984), pp. 44-6.

ROBERTSON, Bruce, *The Art of Paul Sandby*, New Haven, 1985. (Robertson, 1985)

ROGET, J. L., *A History of the 'Old Water-Colour' Society*, 2 Vols., London, 1891.

SANDBY, William, *Thomas and Paul Sandby – Royal Academicians*, London, 1892. (W. A. Sandby, 1892)

STAINTON, Lindsay, *British Landscape Watercolours, 1600–1860*, British Museum, London, 1985.

WILLIAM WESTON GALLERY, *Paul Sandby, Etchings and Aquatints*, London, 1977.

WHITLEY, W. T., *Artists and their Friends in England, 1700–1799*, 2 Vols., London, 1928 (Reprint 1968).

WHITLEY, W. T. *Art in England, 1800–1820*, London, 1930 (Reprint 1973).

WILLIAMS, Iolo, *Early English Watercolours*, London, 1952.

Index